ASPEN PUBLISHERS

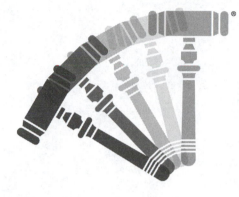

Casenote™ Legal Briefs

INTERNATIONAL LAW

Keyed to Courses Using

Dunoff, Ratner, and Wippman's
International Law: Norms, Actors, Process

Third Edition

Wolters Kluwer
Law & Business

AUSTIN   BOSTON   CHICAGO   NEW YORK   THE NETHERLANDS

© 2011 Aspen Publishers. All Rights Reserved.
www.AspenLaw.com

No part of this publication may be reproduced or transmitted in any form or by any means, electronic or mechanical, including photocopy, recording, or any information storage and retrieval system, without permission in writing from the publisher. Requests for permission to make copies of any part of this publication should be mailed to:

Aspen Publishers
Attn: Permissions Dept.
76 Ninth Avenue, 7th Floor
New York, NY 10011-5201

To contact Customer Care, e-mail customer.service@aspenpublishers.com, call 1-800-234-1660, fax 1-800-901-9075, or mail correspondence to:

Aspen Publishers
Attn: Order Department
P.O. Box 990
Frederick, MD 21705

Printed in the United States of America.

1 2 3 4 5 6 7 8 9 0

ISBN 978-0-7355-8981-0

About Wolters Kluwer Law & Business

Wolters Kluwer Law & Business is a leading provider of research information and workflow solutions in key specialty areas. The strengths of the individual brands of Aspen Publishers, CCH, Kluwer Law International and Loislaw are aligned within Wolters Kluwer Law & Business to provide comprehensive, in-depth solutions and expert-authored content for the legal, professional and education markets.

CCH was founded in 1913 and has served more than four generations of business professionals and their clients. The CCH products in the Wolters Kluwer Law & Business group are highly regarded electronic and print resources for legal, securities, antitrust and trade regulation, government contracting, banking, pension, payroll, employment and labor, and health-care reimbursement and compliance professionals.

Aspen Publishers is a leading information provider for attorneys, business professionals and law students. Written by preeminent authorities, Aspen products offer analytical and practical information in a range of specialty practice areas from securities law and intellectual property to mergers and acquisitions and pension/benefits. Aspen's trusted legal education resources provide professors and students with high-quality, up-to-date and effective resources for successful instruction and study in all areas of the law.

Kluwer Law International supplies the global business community with comprehensive English-language international legal information. Legal practitioners, corporate counsel and business executives around the world rely on the Kluwer Law International journals, loose-leafs, books and electronic products for authoritative information in many areas of international legal practice.

Loislaw is a premier provider of digitized legal content to small law firm practitioners of various specializations. Loislaw provides attorneys with the ability to quickly and efficiently find the necessary legal information they need, when and where they need it, by facilitating access to primary law as well as state-specific law, records, forms and treatises.

Wolters Kluwer Law & Business, a unit of Wolters Kluwer, is headquartered in New York and Riverwoods, Illinois. Wolters Kluwer is a leading multinational publisher and information services company.

Format for the Casenote Legal Brief

Nature of Case: This section identifies the form of action (e.g., breach of contract, negligence, battery), the type of proceeding (e.g., demurrer, appeal from trial court's jury instructions), or the relief sought (e.g., damages, injunction, criminal sanctions).

Fact Summary: This is included to refresh your memory and can be used as a quick reminder of the facts.

Rule of Law: Summarizes the general principle of law that the case illustrates. It may be used for instant recall of the court's holding and for classroom discussion or home review.

Facts: This section contains all relevant facts of the case, including the contentions of the parties and the lower court holdings. It is written in a logical order to give the student a clear understanding of the case. The plaintiff and defendant are identified by their proper names throughout and are always labeled with a (P) or (D).

Palsgraf v. Long Island R.R. Co.

Injured bystander (P) v. Railroad company (D)

N.Y. Ct. App., 248 N.Y. 339, 162 N.E. 99 (1928).

NATURE OF CASE: Appeal from judgment affirming verdict for plaintiff seeking damages for personal injury.

FACT SUMMARY: Helen Palsgraf (P) was injured on R.R.'s (D) train platform when R.R.'s (D) guard helped a passenger aboard a moving train, causing his package to fall on the tracks. The package contained fireworks which exploded, creating a shock that tipped a scale onto Palsgraf (P).

🏛 RULE OF LAW
The risk reasonably to be perceived defines the duty to be obeyed.

FACTS: Helen Palsgraf (P) purchased a ticket to Rockaway Beach from R.R. (D) and was waiting on the train platform. As she waited, two men ran to catch a train that was pulling out from the platform. The first man jumped aboard, but the second man, who appeared as if he might fall, was helped aboard by the guard on the train who had kept the door open so they could jump aboard. A guard on the platform also helped by pushing him onto the train. The man was carrying a package wrapped in newspaper. In the process, the man dropped his package, which fell on the tracks. The package contained fireworks and exploded. The shock of the explosion was apparently of great enough strength to tip over some scales at the other end of the platform, which fell on Palsgraf (P) and injured her. A jury awarded her damages, and R.R. (D) appealed.

ISSUE: Does the risk reasonably to be perceived define the duty to be obeyed?

HOLDING AND DECISION: (Cardozo, C.J.) Yes. The risk reasonably to be perceived defines the duty to be obeyed. If there is no foreseeable hazard to the injured party as the result of a seemingly innocent act, the act does not become a tort because it happened to be a wrong as to another. If the wrong was not willful, the plaintiff must show that the act as to her had such great and apparent possibilities of danger as to entitle her to protection. Negligence in the abstract is not enough upon which to base liability. Negligence is a relative concept, evolving out of the common law doctrine of trespass on the case. To establish liability, the defendant must owe a legal duty of reasonable care to the injured party. A cause of action in tort will lie where harm,

though unintended, could have been averted or avoided by observance of such a duty. The scope of the duty is limited by the range of danger that a reasonable person could foresee. In this case, there was nothing to suggest from the appearance of the parcel or otherwise that the parcel contained fireworks. The guard could not reasonably have had any warning of a threat to Palsgraf (P), and R.R. (D) therefore cannot be held liable. Judgment is reversed in favor of R.R. (D).

DISSENT: (Andrews, J.) The concept that there is no negligence unless R.R. (D) owes a legal duty to take care as to Palsgraf (P) herself is too narrow. Everyone owes to the world at large the duty of refraining from those acts that may unreasonably threaten the safety of others. If the guard's action was negligent as to those nearby, it was also negligent as to those outside what might be termed the "danger zone." For Palsgraf (P) to recover, R.R.'s (D) negligence must have been the proximate cause of her injury, a question of fact for the jury.

▶ ANALYSIS

The majority defined the limit of the defendant's liability in terms of the danger that a reasonable person in defendant's situation would have perceived. The dissent argued that the limitation should not be placed on liability, but rather on damages. Judge Andrews suggested that only injuries that would not have happened but for R.R.'s (D) negligence should be compensable. Both the majority and dissent recognized the policy-driven need to limit liability for negligent acts, seeking, in the words of Judge Andrews, to define a framework "that will be practical and in keeping with the general understanding of mankind." The Restatement (Second) of Torts has accepted Judge Cardozo's view.

Quicknotes

FORESEEABILITY A reasonable expectation that change is the probable result of certain acts or omissions.

NEGLIGENCE Conduct falling below the standard of care that a reasonable person would demonstrate under similar conditions.

PROXIMATE CAUSE The natural sequence of events without which an injury would not have been sustained.

Party ID: Quick identification of the relationship between the parties.

Concurrence/Dissent: All concurrences and dissents are briefed whenever they are included by the casebook editor.

Analysis: This last paragraph gives you a broad understanding of where the case "fits in" with other cases in the section of the book and with the entire course. It is a hornbook-style discussion indicating whether the case is a majority or minority opinion and comparing the principal case with other cases in the casebook. It may also provide analysis from restatements, uniform codes, and law review articles. The analysis will prove to be invaluable to classroom discussion.

Issue: The issue is a concise question that brings out the essence of the opinion as it relates to the section of the casebook in which the case appears. Both substantive and procedural issues are included if relevant to the decision.

Holding and Decision: This section offers a clear and in-depth discussion of the rule of the case and the court's rationale. It is written in easy-to-understand language and answers the issue presented by applying the law to the facts of the case. When relevant, it includes a thorough discussion of the exceptions to the case as listed by the court, any major cites to the other cases on point, and the names of the judges who wrote the decisions.

Quicknotes: Conveniently defines legal terms found in the case and summarizes the nature of any statutes, codes, or rules referred to in the text.

Aspen Publishers is proud to offer *Casenote Legal Briefs*—continuing thirty years of publishing America's best-selling legal briefs.

Casenote Legal Briefs are designed to help you save time when briefing assigned cases. Organized under convenient headings, they show you how to abstract the basic facts and holdings from the text of the actual opinions handed down by the courts. Used as part of a rigorous study regimen, they can help you spend more time analyzing and critiquing points of law than on copying bits and pieces of judicial opinions into your notebook or outline.

Casenote Legal Briefs should never be used as a substitute for assigned casebook readings. They work best when read as a follow-up to reviewing the underlying opinions themselves. Students who try to avoid reading and digesting the judicial opinions in their casebooks or online sources will end up shortchanging themselves in the long run. The ability to absorb, critique, and restate the dynamic and complex elements of case law decisions is crucial to your success in law school and beyond. It cannot be developed vicariously.

Casenote Legal Briefs represents but one of the many offerings in Aspen's Study Aid Timeline, which includes:

- *Casenote Legal Briefs*
- *Emanuel Law Outlines*
- *Examples & Explanations* Series
- *Introduction to Law* Series
- Emanuel *Law in a Flash* Flash Cards
- Emanuel *CrunchTime* Series

Each of these series is designed to provide you with easy-to-understand explanations of complex points of law. Each volume offers guidance on the principles of legal analysis and, consulted regularly, will hone your ability to spot relevant issues. We have titles that will help you prepare for class, prepare for your exams, and enhance your general comprehension of the law along the way.

To find out more about Aspen Study Aid publications, visit us online at *www.AspenLaw.com* or email us at *legaledu@wolterskluwer.com*. We'll be happy to assist you.

Get this Casenote Legal Brief as an AspenLaw Studydesk eBook today!

By returning this form to Aspen Publishers, you will receive a complimentary eBook download of this Casenote Legal Brief and AspenLaw Studydesk productivity software.* Learn more about AspenLaw Studydesk today at *www.AspenLaw.com/Studydesk*.

Name	Phone ( )
Address	**Apt. No.**
City	**State**	**ZIP Code**
Law School	**Graduation Date** Month _____ Year _____

Cut out the UPC found on the lower left corner of the back cover of this book. Staple the UPC inside this box. Only the original UPC from the book cover will be accepted. (No photocopies or store stickers are allowed.)

Attach UPC inside this box.

Email (Print legibly or you may not get access!)

Title of this book (course subject)

ISBN of this book (10- or 13-digit number on the UPC)

Used with which casebook (provide author's name)

Mail the completed form to:

Aspen Publishers, Inc.
Legal Education Division
130 Turner Street, Bldg 3, 4th Floor
Waltham, MA 02453-8901

* Upon receipt of this completed form, you will be emailed a code for the digital download of this book in AspenLaw Studydesk eBook format and a free copy of the software application, which is required to read the eBook.

For a full list of eBook study aids available for AspenLaw Studydesk software and other resources that will help you with your law school studies, visit *www.AspenLaw.com*.

Make a photocopy of this form and your UPC for your records.

For detailed information on the use of the information you provide on this form, please see the PRIVACY POLICY at *www.AspenLaw.com*.

How to Brief a Case

A. Decide on a Format and Stick to It

Structure is essential to a good brief. It enables you to arrange systematically the related parts that are scattered throughout most cases, thus making manageable and understandable what might otherwise seem to be an endless and unfathomable sea of information. There are, of course, an unlimited number of formats that can be utilized. However, it is best to find one that suits your needs and stick to it. Consistency breeds both efficiency and the security that when called upon you will know where to look in your brief for the information you are asked to give.

Any format, as long as it presents the essential elements of a case in an organized fashion, can be used. Experience, however, has led *Casenotes* to develop and utilize the following format because of its logical flow and universal applicability.

NATURE OF CASE: This is a brief statement of the legal character and procedural status of the case (e.g., "Appeal of a burglary conviction").

There are many different alternatives open to a litigant dissatisfied with a court ruling. The key to determining which one has been used is to discover *who is asking this court for what.*

This first entry in the brief should be kept as *short as possible.* Use the court's terminology if you understand it. But since jurisdictions vary as to the titles of pleadings, the best entry is the one that addresses who wants what in this proceeding, not the one that sounds most like the court's language.

RULE OF LAW: A statement of the general principle of law that the case illustrates (e.g., "An acceptance that varies any term of the offer is considered a rejection and counteroffer").

Determining the rule of law of a case is a procedure similar to determining the issue of the case. Avoid being fooled by red herrings; there may be a few rules of law mentioned in the case excerpt, but usually only one is *the* rule with which the casebook editor is concerned. The techniques used to locate the issue, described below, may also be utilized to find the rule of law. Generally, your best guide is simply the chapter heading. It is a clue to the point the casebook editor seeks to make and should be kept in mind when reading every case in the respective section.

FACTS: A synopsis of only the essential facts of the case, i.e., those bearing upon or leading up to the issue.

The facts entry should be a short statement of the events and transactions that led one party to initiate legal proceedings against another in the first place. While some cases conveniently state the salient facts at the beginning of the decision, in other instances they will have to be culled from hiding places throughout the text, even from concurring and dissenting opinions. Some of the "facts" will often be in dispute and should be so noted. Conflicting evidence may be briefly pointed up. "Hard" facts must be included. Both must be *relevant* in order to be listed in the facts entry. It is impossible to tell what is relevant until the entire case is read, as the ultimate determination of the rights and liabilities of the parties may turn on something buried deep in the opinion.

Generally, the facts entry should not be longer than three to five *short* sentences.

It is often helpful to identify the role played by a party in a given context. For example, in a construction contract case the identification of a party as the "contractor" or "builder" alleviates the need to tell that that party was the one who was supposed to have built the house.

It is always helpful, and a good general practice, to identify the "plaintiff" and the "defendant." This may seem elementary and uncomplicated, but, especially in view of the creative editing practiced by some casebook editors, it is sometimes a difficult or even impossible task. Bear in mind that the *party presently* seeking something from this court may not be the plaintiff, and that sometimes only the cross-claim of a defendant is treated in the excerpt. Confusing or misaligning the parties can ruin your analysis and understanding of the case.

ISSUE: A statement of the general legal question answered by or illustrated in the case. For clarity, the issue is best put in the form of a question capable of a "yes" or "no" answer. In reality, the issue is simply the Rule of Law put in the form of a question (e.g., "May an offer be accepted by performance?").

The major problem presented in discerning what is *the* issue in the case is that an opinion usually purports to raise and answer several questions. However, except for rare cases, only one such question is really the issue in the case. Collateral issues not necessary to the resolution of the matter in controversy are handled by the court by language known as *"obiter dictum"* or merely *"dictum."* While dicta may be included later in the brief, they have no place under the issue heading.

To find the issue, ask *who wants what* and then go on to ask *why did that party succeed or fail in getting it.* Once this is determined, the "why" should be turned into a question.

The complexity of the issues in the cases will vary, but in all cases a single-sentence question should sum up the issue. *In a few cases,* there will be two, or even more rarely, three issues of equal importance to the resolution of the case. Each should be expressed in a single-sentence question.

Since many issues are resolved by a court in coming to a final disposition of a case, the casebook editor will reproduce the portion of the opinion containing the issue or issues most relevant to the area of law under scrutiny. A noted law professor gave this advice: "Close the book; look at the title on the cover." Chances are, if it is Property, you need not concern yourself with whether, for example, the federal government's treatment of the plaintiff's land really raises a federal question sufficient to support jurisdiction on this ground in federal court.

The same rule applies to chapter headings designating sub-areas within the subjects. They tip you off as to what the text is designed to teach. The cases are arranged in a casebook to show a progression or development of the law, so that the preceding cases may also help.

It is also most important to remember to *read the notes and questions* at the end of a case to determine what the editors wanted you to have gleaned from it.

HOLDING AND DECISION: This section should succinctly explain the rationale of the court in arriving at its decision. In capsulizing the "reasoning" of the court, it should always include an application of the general rule or rules of law to the specific facts of the case. Hidden justifications come to light in this entry: the reasons for the state of the law, the public policies, the biases and prejudices, those considerations that influence the justices' thinking and, ultimately, the outcome of the case. At the end, there should be a short indication of the disposition or procedural resolution of the case (e.g., "Decision of the trial court for Mr. Smith (P) reversed").

The foregoing format is designed to help you "digest" the reams of case material with which you will be faced in your law school career. Once mastered by practice, it will place at your fingertips the information the authors of your casebooks have sought to impart to you in case-by-case illustration and analysis.

B. Be as Economical as Possible in Briefing Cases

Once armed with a format that encourages succinctness, it is as important to be economical with regard to the time spent on the actual reading of the case as it is to be economical in the writing of the brief itself. This does not mean "skimming" a case. Rather, it means reading the case with an "eye" trained to recognize into which "section" of your brief a particular passage or line fits and having a system for quickly and precisely marking the case so that the passages fitting any one particular part of

the brief can be easily identified and brought together in a concise and accurate manner when the brief is actually written.

It is of no use to simply repeat everything in the opinion of the court; record only enough information to trigger your recollection of what the court said. Nevertheless, an accurate statement of the "law of the case," i.e., the legal principle applied to the facts, is absolutely essential to class preparation and to learning the law under the case method.

To that end, it is important to develop a "shorthand" that you can use to make marginal notations. These notations will tell you at a glance in which section of the brief you will be placing that particular passage or portion of the opinion.

Some students prefer to underline all the salient portions of the opinion (with a pencil or colored underliner marker), making marginal notations as they go along. Others prefer the color-coded method of underlining, utilizing different colors of markers to underline the salient portions of the case, each separate color being used to represent a different section of the brief. For example, blue underlining could be used for passages relating to the rule of law, yellow for those relating to the issue, and green for those relating to the holding and decision, etc. While it has its advocates, the color-coded method can be confusing and time-consuming (all that time spent on changing colored markers). Furthermore, it can interfere with the continuity and concentration many students deem essential to the reading of a case for maximum comprehension. In the end, however, it is a matter of personal preference and style. Just remember, whatever method you use, underlining must be used sparingly or its value is lost.

If you take the marginal notation route, an efficient and easy method is to go along underlining the key portions of the case and placing in the margin alongside them the following "markers" to indicate where a particular passage or line "belongs" in the brief you will write:

N   (NATURE OF CASE)
RL   (RULE OF LAW)
I   (ISSUE)
HL   (HOLDING AND DECISION, relates to
      the RULE OF LAW behind the decision)
HR   (HOLDING AND DECISION, gives the
      RATIONALE or reasoning behind the
      decision)
HA   (HOLDING AND DECISION, APPLIES
      the general principle(s) of law to the facts
      of the case to arrive at the decision)

Remember that a particular passage may well contain information necessary to more than one part of your brief, in which case you simply note that in the margin. If you are using the color-coded underlining method instead of marginal notation, simply make asterisks or checks in the margin next to the passage in question in the colors that indicate the additional sections of the brief where it might be utilized.

The economy of utilizing "shorthand" in marking cases for briefing can be maintained in the actual brief writing process itself by utilizing "law student shorthand" within the brief. There are many commonly used words and phrases for which abbreviations can be substituted in your briefs (and in your class notes also). You can develop abbreviations that are personal to you and which will save you a lot of time. A reference list of briefing abbreviations can be found on page xii of this book.

C. Use Both the Briefing Process and the Brief as a Learning Tool

Now that you have a format and the tools for briefing cases efficiently, the most important thing is to make the time spent in briefing profitable to you and to make the most advantageous use of the briefs you create. Of course, the briefs are invaluable for classroom reference when you are called upon to explain or analyze a particular case. However, they are also useful in reviewing for exams. A quick glance at the fact summary should bring the case to mind, and a rereading of the rule of law should enable you to go over the underlying legal concept in your mind, how it was applied in that particular case, and how it might apply in other factual settings.

As to the value to be derived from engaging in the briefing process itself, there is an immediate benefit that arises from being forced to sift through the essential facts and reasoning from the court's opinion and to succinctly express them in your own words in your brief. The process ensures that you understand the case and the point that it illustrates, and that means you will be ready to absorb further analysis and information brought forth in class. It also ensures you will have something to say when called upon in class. The briefing process helps develop a mental agility for getting to the *gist* of a case and for identifying, expounding on, and applying the legal concepts and issues found there. The briefing process is the mental process on which you must rely in taking law school examinations; it is also the mental process upon which a lawyer relies in serving his clients and in making his living.

acceptance	acp	offer	O
affirmed	aff	offeree	OE
answer	ans	offeror	OR
assumption of risk	a/r	ordinance	ord
attorney	atty	pain and suffering	p/s
beyond a reasonable doubt	b/r/d	parol evidence	p/e
bona fide purchaser	BFP	plaintiff	P
breach of contract	br/k	prima facie	p/f
cause of action	c/a	probable cause	p/c
common law	c/l	proximate cause	px/c
Constitution	Con	real property	r/p
constitutional	con	reasonable doubt	r/d
contract	K	reasonable man	r/m
contributory negligence	c/n	rebuttable presumption	rb/p
cross	x	remanded	rem
cross-complaint	x/c	res ipsa loquitur	RIL
cross-examination	x/ex	respondeat superior	r/s
cruel and unusual punishment	c/u/p	Restatement	RS
defendant	D	reversed	rev
dismissed	dis	Rule Against Perpetuities	RAP
double jeopardy	d/j	search and seizure	s/s
due process	d/p	search warrant	s/w
equal protection	e/p	self-defense	s/d
equity	eq	specific performance	s/p
evidence	ev	statute	S
exclude	exc	statute of frauds	S/F
exclusionary rule	exc/r	statute of limitations	S/L
felony	f/n	summary judgment	s/j
freedom of speech	f/s	tenancy at will	t/w
good faith	g/f	tenancy in common	t/c
habeas corpus	h/c	tenant	t
hearsay	hr	third party	TP
husband	H	third party beneficiary	TPB
injunction	inj	transferred intent	TI
in loco parentis	ILP	unconscionable	uncon
inter vivos	I/v	unconstitutional	unconst
joint tenancy	j/t	undue influence	u/e
judgment	judgt	Uniform Commercial Code	UCC
jurisdiction	jur	unilateral	uni
last clear chance	LCC	vendee	VE
long-arm statute	LAS	vendor	VR
majority view	maj	versus	v
meeting of minds	MOM	void for vagueness	VFV
minority view	min	weight of authority	w/a
Miranda rule	Mir/r	weight of the evidence	w/e
Miranda warnings	Mir/w	wife	W
negligence	neg	with	w/
notice	ntc	within	w/i
nuisance	nus	without	w/o
obligation	ob	without prejudice	w/o/p
obscene	obs	wrongful death	wr/d

Table of Cases

CHAPTER 1

Tracing the Evolution of International Law Through Two Problems

Quick Reference Rules of Law

Case Concerning the Territorial Dispute (Libya/Chad)

Nation disputing its border (P) v. Nation disputing its border (D)

1994 I.C.J. 6 (Feb. 3).

NATURE OF CASE: Proceeding before the International Court of Justice (ICJ) to determine the border between two countries.

FACT SUMMARY: Chad (P) claimed that Libya (D) was occupying its territory, the Aouzou Strip. Libya (D) claimed that the Aouzou Strip belonged to Libya and that a 1955 treaty between Libya and France, Chad's colonial ruler, was not dispositive of the dispute.

🏛 RULE OF LAW
A permanent boundary, once established in a treaty, does not depend for its permanence on the continued existence of the treaty.

FACTS: Chad (P) and Libya (D) lay claim, respectively, to the Aouzou Strip that lies between the two countries. Libya had occupied the Aouzou Strip since 1973, and Chad complained of this occupation. Libya had entered into a treaty in 1955 (the 1955 Treaty) with France, which ruled Chad until 1960. The treaty referenced prior agreements between other countries (Britain and Italy), and Chad claimed that the 1955 Treaty that recognized the validity of these prior agreements continued to bind Libya. Libya claimed that the Treaty was invalid and, in any event, had not been intended to settle all frontier questions. The ICJ determined to the contrary, and the ICJ concluded that the line from a 1919 France-Britain agreement, combined with a line from a France-Italy agreement, determined the border in Chad's favor.

ISSUE: Does a permanent boundary, once established in a treaty, depend for its permanence on the continued existence of the treaty?

HOLDING AND DECISION: [Judge not stated in casebook excerpt.] No. A permanent boundary, once established in a treaty, does not depend for its permanence on the continued existence of the treaty. The 1955 Treaty established the frontier between Libya and Chad. No subsequent treaty, or any act of the Parties called in question this frontier, and, to the contrary, subsequent treaties and acts by the Parties suggested that the existence of this frontier was accepted by the Parties. Chad consistently took the position that its territory included the Aouzou Strip, and took actions consistent with this position, e.g., complaining to the U.N. General Assembly and Security Council that Libya was interfering with its affairs by occupying the Aouzou Strip. Although the 1955 Treaty permits either party to terminate it after 20 years, the Treaty is determinative of the permanent frontier as there was nothing in it to indicate that it was to be temporary. The establishment of the boundary thus has a legal life of its own that is independent of the life of the Treaty; otherwise, the fundamental principle of the stability of boundaries would be vitiated. Thus, the Treaty can cease to exist, but the boundary will continue, absent mutual agreement of the Parties to alter the boundary. Here, the boundary dispute is conclusively and completely determined by the 1955 Treaty, and it is unnecessary to consider the history of the region or the effectiveness of any occupation of the territory in dispute or concepts such as "*terra nullius*" or "spheres of influence."

▶ ANALYSIS

This case is an example of two states resolving a dispute through legal channels and arguments, and entrusting the final resolution of the dispute to an international court. Some alternative legal methods of resolving such a dispute are the use of arbitral tribunals or the entering into of additional treaties.

■■■

Ruling Pertaining to the Differences between France and New Zealand Arising from the *Rainbow Warrior* Affair

Nation v. Nation

26 I.L.M. 1349 (1987).

NATURE OF CASE: Arbitration of issues between France and New Zealand submitted to the UN Secretary-General.

FACT SUMMARY: French agents bombed a Greenpeace ship, *Rainbow Warrior*, which was docked in a New Zealand Harbor, and the two nations submitted issues to the United Nations Secretary-General for resolution.

RULE OF LAW

Where a nation's agents have violated international law and committed acts that are crimes in a second nation, the first nation may be required to provide the second nation with an apology, compensation, assurances that guilty parties will be punished if returned to the first nation, and assurances that no trade sanctions will be levied against the second nation as a result of the affair.

FACTS: On July 10, 1985, several French service agents bombed the Greenpeace ship *Rainbow Warrior*, which was docked in a New Zealand harbor. New Zealand authorities caught two of the agents. Believing the act to be a crime, as well as a violation of international law, New Zealand tried, convicted, and imprisoned the two agents. France sought the immediate return of the two officers. New Zealand sought an apology, compensation for damages for the benefit of Greenpeace and the family of a Dutch crewmember who died in the explosion, assurances that the agents would be imprisoned by the French government if returned, and assurances that France would not engage trade sanctions against New Zealand. The parties agreed to submit the issues to the United Nations Secretary-General for binding resolution.

ISSUE: Where a nation's agents have violated international law and committed acts that are crimes in a second nation, may the first nation be required to provide the second nation with an apology, compensation, assurances that guilty parties will be punished if returned to the first nation, and assurances that no trade sanctions will be levied against the second nation as a result of the affair?

HOLDING AND DECISION: (Javier Perez de Cuellar, UN Secretary-General) Yes. Where a nation's agents have violated international law and committed acts that are crimes in a second nation, the first nation may be required to provide the second nation with an apology, compensation, assurances that guilty parties will be

punished if returned to the first nation, and assurances that no trade sanctions will be levied against the second nation as a result of the affair. First, New Zealand asked for an apology and France agreed to provide one. The Prime Minister of France should therefore convey to the Prime Minister of New Zealand a formal and unqualified apology for the attack. Second, New Zealand asked for compensation for damages resulting from the attack and France agreed to provide it, though the parties disagreed about the appropriate amount. The amount France should pay is $7 million US dollars, which is a compromise amount between New Zealand's demand of $9 million and France's offer of $4 million. Third, the two officers should be returned to France, but should be transferred to French military authorities on a military facility on an isolated island outside of Europe for three years. They should be prohibited from leaving the island except with mutual consent of both governments, and the French government should provide New Zealand with assurances that the agents are still imprisoned every three months. If New Zealand asks, a third party should be allowed to visit the facility to verify that the two agents are imprisoned. Finally, while France denied that it had raised trade issues to leverage its position in the negotiations, France also agreed to not oppose imports of New Zealand butter into the United Kingdom in 1987 and 1988, or to take any measure that might stall the implementation of the agreement between New Zealand and the European Economic Community on Trade in mutton, lamb, and goat meat. Finally, an agreement should be drafted that implements all of these rulings, and that requires both parties to submit to arbitration differences that may arise about the implementation of these rulings.

ANALYSIS

Note that neither of the French agents spent the assigned three years in a French military base on an island. Without New Zealand's consent, both were moved from the island before the end of the three-year term for different reasons. New Zealand pressed for arbitration, and the panel found in favor of New Zealand, but because the three-year period they were to serve had passed, France's obligations had ended.

Continued on next page.

Quicknotes

ARBITRATION An alternative resolution process where a dispute is heard and decided by a neutral third party, rather than through legal proceedings.

SANCTIONS A penalty imposed in order to ensure compliance with a statute or regulation.

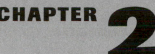
Making Law in a Decentralized System

Quick Reference Rules of Law

Reservations to the Convention on the Prevention and Punishment of the Crime of Genocide

[Parties not identified.]

1951 I.C.J. 15 (May 28).

NATURE OF CASE: Proceeding before the International Court of Justice (ICJ) to determine the permissibility of reservations to a convention.

FACT SUMMARY: The Genocide Convention was promulgated in 1948, and the ICJ was asked to determine whether reservations to the Convention were permissible.

🏛 RULES OF LAW
(1) If a party to the Genocide Convention objects to a reservation that it considers to be incompatible with the Convention's objective and purpose, it can consider that the reserving state is not a party to the Convention.
(2) If a party to the Convention accepts a reservation as compatible with the Convention's objective and purpose, it can consider that the reserving state is a party to the Convention.

FACTS: The Genocide Convention was promulgated in 1948. Several states had indicated their intent to ratify the Convention with reservations concerning various articles, especially Article 9 relating to the reference of disputes to the ICJ. The ICJ was asked to determine whether reservations to the Convention were permissible.

ISSUE:
(1) If a party to the Convention objects to a reservation that it considers to be incompatible with the Convention's object and purpose, can it consider that the reserving state is not a party to the Convention?
(2) If a party to the Convention accepts a reservation as compatible with the Convention's object and purpose, can it consider that the reserving state is a party to the Convention?

HOLDING AND DECISION: [Judge not stated in casebook excerpt.] It is a recognized principle that no state can be bound to a reservation without its agreement and that no state can unilaterally impede the purpose and object of a convention. These principles led to the notion that no reservation could be valid unless all contracting parties accepted it without exception. However, with regard to humanitarian conventions, such as the Genocide Convention, a more flexible principle is required. This is because in such a convention, the states do not have any interests of their own, but instead have a common interest, namely the achievement of the Convention's purposes. Therefore, in such a convention, maintaining a balance between contractual rights and duties is inapposite. Applying these considerations to objections to reservations leads to several conclusions. First, it was the intent of the states that adopted the Convention that as many states as possible should participate, and, therefore, it was not the intent that an objection to a minor reservation should result in the complete exclusion from the Convention of any state—it was not the intent of the contracting parties to sacrifice the goals of the Convention for a "vain desire" to maximize the number of participants. It follows that the compatibility of a reservation with the "object and purpose" of the Convention is the criterion by which a state must decide whether to make a reservation or whether to object to such a reservation. Each state must decide for itself whether a reservation is valid. (1) Therefore, if a state deems the reservation to be invalid, as measured by this criterion, it can consider the reserving state not to be a party to the Convention. (2) Conversely, if the state deems the reservation to be valid, i.e., compatible with the object and purpose of the Convention, it can consider the reserving state to be a party to the Convention.

DISSENT: (Guerrero, J.) The majority's rule is unworkable. First, it leaves unresolved the core issue of whether all of the Convention's enforcement articles are part of the Convention's object and purpose. Second, under the majority's rule, there can be no certainty to the status of a reserving state because the admissibility of any reservation that has been objected to is left to the subjective determination of individual states. This status can only be objectively resolved when the question of compatibility with the Convention's object and purpose is decided judicially—but it is not a foregone conclusion that this issue will ever be brought before a court. Moreover, a judicial resolution of this issue could alter objecting states' assessment of the compatibility of the reservation, thus creating more confusion and uncertainty. In the case of humanitarian Conventions such as the Genocide Convention, it is even more important to have all the states in agreement in order to attain the Convention's humanitarian goals, and it is, therefore, in the interest of the international community to adhere to the rule that the consent of all parties is required for any reservation to a multilateral convention.

▌ ANALYSIS

Despite the dissenters' concerns, the Vienna Convention on Treaties adopted much of the majority's approach to treaty reservations, making it applicable to all treaties, and not just humanitarian treaties such as the Genocide Convention.

■■■

The Paquete Habana

Shipowners (P) v. Shipowners (D)

175 U.S. 677 (1900).

NATURE OF CASE: Appeal from decree of condemnation and sale.

FACT SUMMARY: After a final decree of condemnation and sale of the Paquete Habana (D) and the Lola (D), two Spanish ships engaged in fishing off the coast of Cuba, the owners appealed on the ground that this class of fishing vessels was exempt from seizure as prizes of war.

🏛 RULE OF LAW
Under international law, coastal fishing vessels, pursuing their vocation of catching and bringing in fresh fish, have been recognized as exempt, with their cargoes and crews, from capture as prizes of war.

FACTS: Both the Paquete Habana (D) and the Lola (D) were fishing vessels, running in and out of Cuba and regularly engaged in fishing on the coast of Cuba. The national registry, the owners, and the commanders of the Paquete Habana (D) and the Lola (D) were Spanish. Until stopped by the blocking squadron of the United States as part of the military strategy of the Spanish-American War, neither the Paquete Habana (D) nor the Lola (D) had any knowledge of the existence of the war, or of any blockade. Both, the fishing vessels were brought to the United States and subject in the district court to condemnation proceedings as prizes of war. A final decree of condemnation and sale was entered, the district court not being satisfied that as a matter of law, without any ordinance, treaty or proclamation, fishing vessels of this class are exempt from seizure. The owners of the Paquete Habana (D) and the Lola (D) appealed, and the United States Supreme Court granted certiorari.

ISSUE: Under international law, are coastal fishing vessels, pursuing their vocation of catching and bringing in fresh fish, recognized as exempt, with their cargoes and crews, from capture as prizes of war?

HOLDING AND DECISION: (Gray, J.) Yes. Under international law, coastal fishing vessels, pursuing their vocation of catching and bringing in fresh fish, have been recognized as exempt, with their cargoes and crews, from capture as prizes of war. This rule developed from ancient usage among civilized nations, and gradually ripened into a rule of international law. International law is part of the law of the United States, and must be ascertained and administered by the courts of justice of appropriate jurisdiction, as often as questions of right depending upon it are duly presented. The rule of international law concerning fishing vessels is one which prize courts are bound to take judicial notice of, and to give effect to, in the absence of any treaty or other public act of their own government in relation to the matter. In the case at bar the Paquete Habana (D) and the Lola (D) were proved to be coastal fishing vessels and their cargoes consisted of fresh fish which were brought on board and kept and sold alive. Therefore, since there are no treaties or public acts of the United States to the contrary, this Court declares that the capture of these vessels was unlawful and the order of the lower court is reversed with all the proceeds restored to the claimant.

▶ ANALYSIS

In many national legal systems, parts of the constitution provide a justification for the application of customary international law. In fact, many national constitutions have provisions which acknowledge the nation's acceptance of the principles of international law and their application to relations among nations.

■▬■

Interlocutory Award in Case Concerning SEDCO, Inc. v. National Iranian Oil Company and the Islamic Republic of Iran

Private corporation (P) v. Expropriating nation (D)

Iran-United States Claims Tribunal, 10 Iran-U.S. Cl. Rep. 180 (1986).

NATURE OF CASE: Arbitral proceeding to determine the standard of compensation to be applied in cases where a nation expropriates a private interest.

FACT SUMMARY: [The Islamic Republic of Iran (Iran) (D) expropriated a private interest held by SEDCO (P), a corporation, in an oil company.] SEDCO (P) claimed in arbitration that it was entitled to "full" compensation by virtue of customary international law. Iran claimed that full compensation was not the appropriate standpoint under customary international law.

RULE OF LAW

A nation that expropriates a private interest must provide compensation equivalent to the full value of the property taken.

FACTS: [Iran (D) expropriated SEDCO's (P) interest in SEDIRAN, an oil drilling company. SEDCO (P) was the subsidiary of a U.S. corporation. The United States and Iran (D) agreed to settle commercial disputes by arbitration through a special arbitral tribunal, the Iran-United States Claims Tribunal, and SEDCO's (P) claim was brought before this tribunal.] SEDCO (P) claimed it was entitled to "full" compensation under international law, where full compensation for an ongoing business like SEDIRAN included not only net assets but also goodwill and future earnings. Iran (D) claimed that the standard of compensation should be the net book value of the company, assessed with unjust enrichment as the guiding principle.

ISSUE: Must a nation that expropriates a private interest provide compensation equivalent to the full value of the property taken?

HOLDING AND DECISION: [Arbitrator not stated in casebook excerpt.] Yes. A nation that expropriates a private interest must provide compensation equivalent to the full value of the property taken. Full compensation, equivalent to the full value of the property taken, was the compensation standard before World War II. Since then, it has been difficult to ascertain the current customary international law standard of compensation because current practice—e.g., lump sum payments—can be greatly inspired by nonjudicial considerations, and, therefore, it is difficult to determine from such practice whether the states involved believe their practice is required by international law (*opinio juris*). Proponents of the argument that the full compensation standard has been eroded point to resolutions and declarations of the U.N. General Assembly, but such resolutions are not directly binding on states and are generally not evidence of customary international law, except in certain circumstances. One resolution that may serve as evidence of the erosion in customary international law of the full compensation standard, Resolution 1803 on Permanent Sovereignty over Natural Resources (Resolution 1803), is limited to cases involving systematic large-scale nationalization, as where an entire industry or natural resource is expropriated. That is not the circumstance here, however. In cases of discrete expropriations, such as occurred here, there is overwhelming support from international tribunals and legal writers for the conclusion that the full compensation standard is appropriate, regardless of the legality of the expropriation itself.

ANALYSIS

Implicit in this decision is that case law and legal scholarship can establish the *opinio juris*—the notion that state practice becomes law only when states follow it out of a sense of legal obligation—necessary to find customary law. Since such legal case law or precedent provide only the inference of the subjective element of customary law, in theory, the tribunal could have found such an inference in the General Assembly resolutions adduced by Iran (D), even if finding that such resolutions do not constitute direct evidence of customary law.

Award on the Merits in Dispute Between Texaco Overseas Petroleum Company/California Asiatic Oil Company and the Government of the Libyan Arab Republic

[Parties not identified.]

17 I.L.M. 1 (1978).

NATURE OF CASE: Consideration by an arbitrator of the role of international law in disputes over ownership rights in oil.

FACT SUMMARY: Three resolutions were supported by a majority of members of the United Nations, but provisions in two of them were not supported by any of the developed countries with market economies.

🏛 RULE OF LAW
To be legally binding, United Nations Resolutions must be accepted by a majority of member states representing all of the various groups, including those Western members with market economies, as well as Third World members.

FACTS: Three resolutions [the content of which are not stated in the casebook excerpt] were supported by a majority of members of the United Nations, but two of them were not supported by any of the developed countries with market economies.

ISSUE: To be legally binding, must United Nations Resolutions be accepted by a majority of member states representing all of the various groups, including those Western members with market economies, as well as Third World members?

HOLDING AND DECISION: [Dupuy, René-Jean.] Yes. To be legally binding, United Nations Resolutions must be accepted by a majority of member states representing all of the various groups, including those Western members with market economies, as well as Third World members. To determine the legal validity of the UN Resolutions, the tribunal must distinguish between those provisions expressing rights upon which the states have agreed, and those provisions introducing new principles that were rejected by certain representative groups of states, which have only limited value in the eyes of the states that have adopted them, and no value to those that do not adopt them. When the community of nations agrees upon a provision within a resolution, it confirms a custom among the members by formulating it and specifying its scope. Here, the community supported Resolution 1803, which in substance conforms to international law. But even though Resolutions 3171 and 3281 were also adopted by a majority of members, one paragraph concerning nationalization, which disregarded the role of international law, was not consented to by the most important Western countries, and caused a number of developing countries to abstain. The latter provisions do not have legal value.

▶ ANALYSIS

Almost twenty years earlier, Libya had granted "deeds of concession" to oil companies willing to drill for oil in Libya. Libya's desire to change the terms of the agreements in order to enjoy greater profit—and to protest U.S. support for Israel—prompted Libya to nationalize the property and interests of nine of the international oil companies located in Libya, including a Texaco subsidiary and a Standard Oil subsidiary. The arbitrator found that Libya was obligated to honor the terms of the deeds of concession.

The Traditional Actors: States and International Organizations

Quick Reference Rules of Law

Case Concerning the Frontier Dispute (Burkina Faso v. Mali)

Nation disputing its border (P) v. Nation disputing its border (D)

1986 I.C.J. 554 (Dec. 22).

NATURE OF CASE: Proceeding before the International Court of Justice (ICJ) to determine the border between two countries.

FACT SUMMARY: [Burkina Faso (P) and Mali (D) disagreed on the location of parts of their borders and sought resolution of their dispute.]

🏛 RULE OF LAW
The principle of *uti possidetis* is a general rule of law applicable to any decolonization.

FACTS: [Burkina Faso (P) and Mali (D), two African nations, prior to their independence had been separate French colonies. They disagreed on the location of parts of their borders and sought resolution of their dispute in accordance with the principle of *uti possidetis*.] This principle fixes borders according to pre-independence colonial borders—borders between imperial domains and administrative borders within imperial domains.

ISSUE: Is the principle of *uti possidetis* a general rule of law applicable to any decolonization?

HOLDING AND DECISION [DICTUM]:
[Judge not stated in casebook excerpt.] Yes. The principle of *uti possidetis* is a general rule of law applicable to any decol-onization. The principle of *uti possidetis* is not a special rule that pertains to only one specific system of international law. It is a general rule that inheres in the process of a nation obtaining independence, wherever that may occur, and its purpose is to prevent fighting over borders after the administering power leaves. The adoption by African nations of this principle does not signify that it is merely a practice contributing to the creation of a principle of customary international law, limited to Africa, but that it is the application in Africa of a rule of general scope. Although this principle seems at first to conflict with the principle of self-determination, the maintenance of the territorial status quo in Africa can be seen as the best way to preserve the independence that people have struggled to achieve. Because *uti possidetis* fosters the security and stability necessary to maintaining independence, it complements people's right to self-determination. This principle fixes borders according to pre-independence colonial borders—borders between imperial domains and administrative borders within imperial domains.

▶ ANALYSIS

Despite the fact that colonial borders had been drawn with no regard for the will of the people who were affected by the borders, or for preexisting boundaries of tribal or ethnic entities, most African nations continued to use these borders after achieving independence. As this opinion suggests, adhering to the colonial borders was the preferred method of obviating dissension and attempts at dividing the African states that would have threatened the states' nascent independence.

■=■

Reference re Secession of Quebec

[Parties not identified.]

[1998] 2 S.C.R. 217.

NATURE OF CASE: Advisory opinion regarding self-determination in relation to separatist movements.

FACT SUMMARY: [French-speaking residents of Quebec called for secession from Canada.]

🏛 RULE OF LAW
A peoples' right to self-determination cannot be said to ground a right to unilateral secession.

FACTS: [For many years, many French-speaking residents of Quebec called for secession from Canada, but referenda among Quebec's citizens never showed a majority in favor of secession. A referendum in October 1995, however, did result in only 50.6 percent of the population against independence compared to 49.4 percent in favor. In response to a request by the Canadian Parliament, the Supreme Court of Canada addressed the legality of unilateral secession under both the Canadian Constitution and international law.]

ISSUE: Can a peoples' right to self-determination be said to ground a right to unilateral secession?

HOLDING AND DECISION: [Judge not stated in casebook excerpt.] No. A peoples' right to self-determination cannot be said to ground a right to unilateral secession. The international law principle of self-determination has evolved within a framework of respect for the territorial integrity of existing states. The right to external self-determination has only been granted to peoples under colonial rule or foreign occupation, based on the assumption that both are entities inherently distinct from the colonialist power and the occupant power. External self-determination has also been bestowed upon peoples totally frustrated in their efforts to exercise internally their rights to self-determinism. In this case, Quebec is neither a colony nor a foreign-occupied land. Further, the people of Quebec have not been victims of attacks on their physical existence or integrity or of massive human rights violations. Quebecers are equitably represented in legislative, executive, and judicial institutions; occupy prominent positions within the government of Canada; and enjoy the freedom to pursue their political, economic, social and cultural development.

▌ ANALYSIS

The *Reference re Secession of Quebec* leaves open the possibility that the international law right of self-determination could entail secession as a "last resort" in cases of especially severe oppression in which other channels for exercising internal self-determination had been "totally frustrated."

■■■■

Reparation for Injuries Suffered in the Service of the United Nations

[Parties not identified.]

1949 I.C.J. 174 (Apr. 11).

NATURE OF CASE: Advisory opinion.

FACT SUMMARY: [When the United Nation's mediator was assassinated, this raised the issues of whether the United Nations could seek damages suffered by the organization and whether it could bring claims for its agent's heirs.]

🏛 RULE OF LAW
The United Nations has the capacity to bring an international claim against a country that causes an agent of the United Nations to suffer an injury in the performance of his duties with a view to obtaining the reparation due in respect of the damage caused to the United Nations or to the victim or persons entitled through him.

FACTS: [After war broke out between Israel and the Arab states following Israel's declaration of independence in 1948, the Secretary-General appointed Count Folke Bernadotte of Sweden to mediate a ceasefire between the parties. On September 16, 1948, Bernadotte's car was blown up in Jerusalem. The mediator and a French observer were killed. Jewish extremists were suspected, but none was ever tried by Israel. This raised the question of whether the United Nations could seek damages suffered by the organization and whether it could bring claims for its agent's heirs.]

ISSUE: Does the United Nations have the capacity to bring an international claim against a country that causes an agent of the United Nations to suffer an injury in the performance of his duties with a view to obtaining the reparation due in respect of the damage caused to the United Nations or to the victim or persons entitled through him?

HOLDING AND DECISION: [Judge not stated in casebook excerpt.] Yes. The United Nations has the capacity to bring an international claim against a country that causes an agent of the United Nations to suffer an injury in the performance of his duties with a view to obtaining the reparation due in respect of the damage caused to the United Nations or to the victim or persons entitled through him. The damage means exclusively damage caused to the interests of the Organization itself, to its administrative machine, to its property and assets and to the interests of which it is guardian. With respect to damages caused the victim or persons entitled through him, the Charter does not expressly confer the capacity to include such claim for reparation. However, in order that its agents may perform their duties satisfactorily, they must feel that their protection is assured by the Organization.

For that purpose, it is necessary when an infringement occurs that the Organization should be able to call upon the responsible state to remedy its default, and to obtain reparation for the damage that it might have caused the agent.

▶ ANALYSIS

The court states that the same conclusion applies whether or not the Defendant State is a member of the United Nations. If competing interests arise between the defendant's national state and the United Nations, there is no rule assigning priority to one over the other, so the court states that goodwill and common sense must apply.

■━■

Quicknotes

AGENT An individual who has the authority to act on behalf of another.

■━■

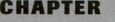
The Challenge of Non-State Actors

Quick Reference Rules of Law

Crosby, Secretary of Administration and Finance of Massachusetts v. National Foreign Trade Council

State official (P) v. Industry group (D)

530 U.S. 363 (2000).

NATURE OF CASE: Appeal from decision that a state statute that prohibits the state from doing business with companies that do business with a certain country unconstitutionally infringes on the federal government's foreign affairs powers.

FACT SUMMARY: Massachusetts (P) had a law that restricted its agencies from purchasing goods and services from companies doing business with Burma. The National Foreign Trade Council (NFTC) (D), an industry group that included companies covered by Massachusetts' "Burma law," argued that the statute unconstitutionally infringed on the federal government's foreign affairs powers.

🏛 RULE OF LAW
A state statute that prohibits the state from doing business with companies that do business with a certain country unconstitutionally infringes on the federal government's foreign affairs powers under the Supremacy Clause.

FACTS: Massachusetts (P) had a law that restricted its agencies from purchasing goods and services from companies doing business with Burma. The National Foreign Trade Council (NFTC) (D), an industry group that included companies covered by Massachusetts' "Burma law," brought suit in federal District Court, arguing that the statute unconstitutionally infringed on the federal government's foreign affairs powers. The district court agreed with NFTC (D), the court of appeals affirmed, and the Supreme Court granted review.

ISSUE: Does a state statute that prohibits the state from doing business with companies that do business with a certain country unconstitutionally infringe on the federal government's foreign affairs powers under the Supremacy Clause?

HOLDING AND DECISION: (Souter, J.) Yes. (III.) A state statute that prohibits the state from doing business with companies that do business with a certain country unconstitutionally infringes on the federal government's foreign affairs powers under the Supremacy Clause. Federal law preempts state law where Congress intended federal law to "occupy the field" or to the extent that the state law conflicts with federal law or interferes with Congress's objectives. (III.A) Congress expressly provided the President with statutory authority to impose sanctions on Burma, and to waive those sanctions in the interest of national security. It is this "plenitude of Executive authority" that controls the

issue of preemption here. Congress would not have gone to such great lengths to empower the President in this regard if it had been willing to compromise his effectiveness by subjecting such power to state or local laws. Here, the Massachusetts (P) law would do exactly that, i.e., undermine the President's power in this area by making it impossible for him to curtail all economic sanctions against Burma if he saw fit to do so.

(III.B) The state statute conflicts with the federal law by penalizing individuals and conduct that Congress has explicitly exempted or excluded from sanctions. The state's argument, that there is no real conflict between the state and federal statutes because their end is the same and because some companies can comply with both statutes, does not render the actual conflict irrelevant. A common end does not necessarily neutralize conflicting means, as the state act conflicts with the federal decision about how much economic pressure should be used; the inconsistency of sanctions undermines the federal "calibration of force."

(III.C) The state act conflicts with the President's role as spokesperson for the U.S among the world's nations in developing a comprehensive multilateral strategy to bring democracy and improved human rights to Burma, and undermines his diplomatic efficacy. By its very existence, the state act compromises the President's ability to speak for the United States with one voice in dealing with other nations. This is supported by a number of formal protests and complaints about the state act from U.S. trading partners and allies.

(IV.) Massachusetts' (P) argument that Congress's failure to expressly preempt the state act implies permission is unconvincing because the existence of conflict under the Supremacy Clause does not depend on express preemption. Also, Congress's intent cannot be gleaned from its ambiguous silence.

(V.) For all these reasons, the state act is preempted and its application is unconstitutional.

▶ ANALYSIS

This case stands for the proposition that conflict preemption may be found even when both the federal and state laws share a common goal, if the state law interferes with, or poses obstacles to, the methods by which the federal statute is designed to reach its goal. Such "obstacle" preemption is not limited to cases involving international relations.

■■■

Continued on next page.

Quicknotes

PLENARY Unlimited and open; as broad as a given situation may require.

PREEMPTION Doctrine holding that matters of national interest take precedence over matters of local interest; the federal law takes precedence over state law.

SUPREMACY CLAUSE Article VI of the U.S. Constitution, which provides that federal action must prevail over inconsistent state action.

■━■

American Insurance Association v. Garamendi, Insurance Commissioner, State of California

Insurance association v. State of California

539 U.S. 396 (2003).

NATURE OF CASE: Appeal to Supreme Court by insurance association and United States as amicus curiae of ruling in favor of the state of California.

FACT SUMMARY: [A California law required insurance companies (P) doing business in the state (D) to disclose prior issuance of Holocaust-era insurance policies in Europe. It was claimed that this state law interfered with U.S. policy—but not legislation—in this area.]

🏛 RULE OF LAW
The likelihood that state legislation will produce something more than incidental effect on foreign affairs requires preemption of the state law by national policy, even when there is no affirmative federal activity in the subject area of the state law, and therefore no showing of conflict.

FACTS: [In the mid-1990s, the U.S. and German governments negotiated the German Foundation Agreement. Under the Agreement Germany and German companies set up a 10-billion Deutschmark foundation to compensate Holocaust victims. That foundation worked with a private organization, the International Commission on Holocaust Era Insurance Claims (ICHEIC), comprised of various Holocaust survivor groups, European insurance companies, U.S. state insurance commissioners, and the government of Israel. ICHEIC negotiated with European insurance companies to get access to information on unpaid policies and settled claims of some survivors. The United States concluded similar agreements with Austria and France. The United States promised to use its "best efforts" to ensure that state and local governments would allow the foundation to serve as the exclusive mechanism for resolving claims. California passed a law, the Holocaust Victim Insurance Relief Act (HVIRA), which required insurance companies (P) doing business in the California (D) to disclose prior issuance of Holocaust-era insurance policies in Europe.]

ISSUE: Does the likelihood that state legislation will produce something more than incidental effect on foreign affairs require preemption of the state law by national policy, even when there is no affirmative federal activity in the subject area of the state law, and therefore no showing of conflict?

HOLDING AND DECISION: (Souter, J.) Yes. The likelihood that state legislation will produce something more than incidental effect on foreign affairs requires preemption of the state law by national policy, even when there is no affirmative federal activity in the subject area of

the state law, and therefore no showing of conflict. California's provision of regulatory sanctions to compel disclosure of certain information by insurance companies contravenes national foreign policy encouraging European governments and companies to volunteer disclosure. And even if there were no conflict here, California's interest in vindicating the claims of Holocaust survivors living in the state is weak compared with the national interest in vindicating the claims of Holocaust survivors throughout the country. California seeks to use "an iron fist" where the President has consistently chosen "kid gloves."

DISSENT: (Ginsberg, J.) Because no executive agreement or other formal expression of foreign policy disapproves state disclosure laws like the one at issue here, California's law should be left intact. The notion of "dormant foreign affairs preemption" should be limited to situations in which the state law criticizes foreign governments. The state law at issue here takes no position on any foreign government. In addition, declining to invalidate the California state law in this case would reserve foreign affairs preemption for circumstances where the President, acting under statutory or constitutional authority, has spoken clearly on the issue.

▶ *ANALYSIS*

This case essentially preempts any state law that deals in any way with international relations. The majority's broad strokes prevent the formulation of a rule that outlines what a state may and may not do in a state law that has any possible bearing on international relations.

■▬■

Quicknotes

AMICUS CURIAE A third party, not implicated in the suit, which seeks to file a brief containing information for the court's consideration in conformity with its position.

■▬■

International Law in the Domestic Arena

Quick Reference Rules of Law

Missouri v. Holland

State (P) v. Game warden (D)

252 U.S. 416 (1920).

NATURE OF CASE: Appeal from dismissal of bill of equity action.

FACT SUMMARY: Missouri (P) brought this suit to prevent Holland (D), a game warden of the United States, from attempting to enforce the Migratory Bird Treaty Act on the ground that the statute was an unconstitutional interference with the rights reserved to the states by the Tenth Amendment.

RULE OF LAW

Treaties are the supreme law of the land when made under the authority of the United States.

FACTS: This is a bill in equity brought by the state of Missouri (P) to prevent Holland (D), a game warden of the United States, from attempting to enforce the Migratory Bird Treaty Act, the enactment statute of a treaty between the United States and Great Britain proclaimed by the President. The grounds of the bill is that the statute is an unconstitutional interference with the rights reserved to the states by the Tenth Amendment, and that the acts of Holland (D) done and threatened under that authority invade the sovereign right of the State of Missouri (P) and contravene its will manifested in statutes. A motion to dismiss was sustained by the district court on the ground that the act of Congress is constitutional. The United States Supreme Court granted certiorari.

ISSUE: Are treaties the supreme law of the land when made under the authority of the United States?

HOLDING AND DECISION: (Holmes, J.) Yes. Treaties are the supreme law of the land when made under the authority of the United States. It is contended that a treaty cannot be valid if it infringes the Constitution, that there are limits, therefore, to the treaty-making power, and that one such limit is that what an act of Congress could not do unaided, in derogation of the powers reserved to the states, a treaty cannot do. Although it is true acts of Congress are the supreme law of the land only when made in pursuance of the Constitution, treaties are declared to be so when made under the authority of the United States. Furthermore, valid treaties are as binding within the territorial limits of the states as they are elsewhere throughout the dominion of the United States. Since the Migratory Bird Treaty Act was made pursuant to a treaty between the United States and Canada, its provisions are the supreme law of the land and binding on the State of Missouri. The treaty and the statute must be upheld. The decree of the lower court is affirmed.

ANALYSIS

Justice Sutherland, in discussing the foreign affairs power in *United States v. Curtiss-Wright Export Corp.*, 299 U.S. 304 (1936), stated that as a result of the separation from Great Britain by the colonies acting as a unit, the powers of external sovereignty passed from the Crown not to the colonies severally, but to the colonies in their collective and corporate capacity as the United States. Even before the Declaration, the colonies were a unit in foreign affairs, and the powers to make treaties and maintain diplomatic relations, if they had never been mentioned in the Constitution, would have vested in the federal government as necessary concomitants of nationality.

Quicknotes

DECLARATORY JUDGMENT An adjudication by the courts which grants not relief but is binding over the legal status of the parties involved in the dispute.

EQUITY Fairness; justice; the determination of a matter consistent with principles of fairness and not in strict compliance with rules of law.

JURISDICTION The authority of a court to hear and declare judgment in respect to a particular matter.

TENTH AMENDMENT The tenth amendment to the United States Constitution reserving those powers therein, not expressly delegated to the federal government or prohibited to the states, to the states or to the people.

TREATY An agreement between two or more nations for the benefit of the general public.

Reid v. Covert

[Government agent (P)] v. Soldier's civilian spouse residing abroad (D)

354 U.S. 1 (1957).

NATURE OF CASE: Appeal from denial of a writ of habeas corpus.

FACT SUMMARY: Mrs. Covert (D) was tried by a court-martial for the murder of her husband, a sergeant in the Air Force, while both were residing at an airbase in England, under Article 118 of the Uniform Code of Military Justice.

RULE OF LAW
Civilian dependents accompanying soldiers on active duty overseas cannot constitutionally be subjected to military court-martial for offenses committed overseas, despite treaties or executive agreements to the contrary.

FACTS: Mrs. Covert (D) allegedly killed her husband, an Air Force sergeant, at an airbase in England. Mrs. Covert (D), who was not a member of the armed services, was residing with her husband on the base at the time. Mrs. Covert (D) was tried by a court-martial for murder under Article 118 of the Uniform Code of Military Justice (UCMJ). The court-martial asserted jurisdiction under Article 2 of the UCMJ, which provides that, subject to any treaties or agreements to which the United States is a party, all persons serving with or accompanying the armed forces overseas are subject to the Code. Mrs. Covert (D) was found guilty and sentenced to life imprisonment. Mrs. Covert (D) petitioned for a rehearing. At the time of Mrs. Covert's (D) alleged offense an executive agreement was in effect between the United States and Great Britain that permitted United States military courts to exercise exclusive jurisdiction over offenses committed in Britain by servicemen and their dependents. Mrs. Covert (D) sought a writ of habeas corpus. [The procedural posture of the case is omitted from the casebook extract.]

ISSUE: Can civilian dependents accompanying soldiers on active duty overseas constitutionally be subjected to military court-martial for offenses committed overseas, despite treaties or executive agreements to the contrary?

HOLDING AND DECISION: (Black, J.) No. Civilian dependents accompanying soldiers on active duty overseas cannot constitutionally be subjected to military court-martial for offenses committed overseas, despite treaties or executive agreements to the contrary. No agreement with a foreign nation can confer power on the Congress, or on any other branch of government, that is free from the restraints of the Constitution. The supremacy of the Constitution over treaties has long been recognized, and there is nothing in the language of the Supremacy Clause that intimates that the treaties and laws enacted pursuant to them do not have to comply with the provisions of the Constitution. Given that treaties can be nullified by subsequent statutes to the extent they are inconsistent, it would be completely anomalous to say that a treaty need not comply with the Constitution when such an agreement can be overridden by a statute that must conform to that instrument. Military trials for civilian dependents, accompanying soldiers on active duty overseas, would deprive civilians of the protections of Section 2 of Article III and the Fifth and Sixth Amendments, which require that crimes be tried by a jury after indictment by a grand jury. Since the court-martial of Mrs. Covert (D) did not meet these requirements, it was not constitutionally permitted, even to carry out the United States' treaty obligations to other countries. There is no indication that the founders contemplated setting up a rival system of military courts to compete with civilian courts for jurisdiction over civilians who might have some contact or relationship with the armed forces. [The outcome of the case is not indicated in the casebook extract.]

ANALYSIS

The Supreme Court stated in this opinion that the idea that the relatives of soldiers could be denied a jury trial in a court of law and instead be tried by court-martial under the guise of regulating the armed forces would have seemed incredible to the Founding Fathers, in whose lifetime the right of the military to try soldiers for any offenses in time of peace had only been grudgingly conceded.

Quicknotes

EXECUTIVE AGREEMENT An agreement with a foreign nation that is binding on the country, entered into by the President without Senate approval.

SUPREMACY CLAUSE Article VI, Sec. 2, of the Constitution, which provides that federal action must prevail over inconsistent state action.

TREATY An agreement between two or more nations for the benefit of the general public.

Made in the USA Foundation v. United States

Labor organizations (P) v. Federal government (D)

242 F.3d 1300 (11th Cir. 2001).

NATURE OF CASE: Appeal from decision that the North American Free Trade Agreement (NAFTA) is constitutional.

FACT SUMMARY: Labor organizations and Made in the USA Foundation (P) challenged the constitutionality of NAFTA, centering their challenge on the procedures used to approve the multilateral agreement.

RULE OF LAW

The constitutionality of procedures used by Congress to approve international commercial agreements is a nonjusticiable political question.

FACTS: [A group of national and local labor organizations and a group that promoted the purchase of American-made products, Made in the USA Foundation, challenged the constitutionality of NAFTA, centering their challenge on the procedures used to approve the multilateral agreement.] The district court held that NAFTA's passage by simple majorities of both Houses of Congress was constitutionally sound, and the court of appeals granted review.

ISSUE: Is the constitutionality of procedures used by Congress to approve international commercial agreements a nonjusticiable political question?

HOLDING AND DECISION: [Judge not stated in casebook excerpt.] Yes. The constitutionality of procedures used by Congress to approve international commercial agreements is a nonjusticiable political question. The Constitution confers vast powers on the political branches of government—Congress and the President—in the area of foreign policy, and especially in foreign commerce. The President has the power to enter into treaties and appoint and receive ambassadors and other diplomatic personnel, and Congress, in addition to all its war powers, in its entirety (not just the Senate) has authority to regulate commerce with foreign nations. The judicial branch's role in foreign affairs is thus very narrow and the propriety of the exercise of this political power by the other branches in this area is not subject to judicial review. The Constitution does not provide textual guidance as to the procedures that must be adhered to when approving international commercial agreements. In the absence of such guidance, and given Congress's broad powers to regulate foreign commerce, there are no "judicially manageable" standards to determine when an agreement is significant enough to qualify as a "treaty," and be subjected to the Treaty Clause's rigorous procedural requirements. Therefore, the issue of what kinds of agreements require Senate ratification under the Constitution is a nonjusticiable political question.

ANALYSIS

The court said that its decision did not effectively allow the political branches unfettered discretion in determining whether to subject a particular international agreement to the rigors of the Treaty Clause's procedural requirements, but did not specify what limitations there are, in fact, on such discretion.

Dames & Moore v. Regan

Claimant (P) v. Federal government (D)

453 U.S. 654 (1981).

NATURE OF CASE: Review of challenge to executive order nullifying certain judgments against Iran.

FACT SUMMARY: The president, in settlement of the Iran hostage crisis, executed an order nullifying certain judgments against Iran.

🏛 RULE OF LAW
The president may issue an order nullifying judgments against a foreign state.

FACTS: Dames & Moore (P) obtained a favorable judgment in a breach of contract action against the Iranian government. Around the same time, the United States and Iran entered into a resolution of the hostage crisis. Part of this settlement called for arbitration of disputes between U.S. nationals and the Iranian government. Pursuant to this, President Carter issued an executive order invalidating all unexecuted judgments against Iran and releasing all attachments and garnishments. Dames & Moore (P) challenged the validity of this order. The district court upheld the order, and the Supreme Court granted expedited review.

ISSUE: May the president issue an order nullifying judgments against a foreign state?

HOLDING AND DECISION: (Rehnquist, J.) Yes. The president may issue an order nullifying judgments against a foreign state. The president may act only within authority granted by the Constitution or by Congress. There is no specific authority from Congress giving the president the power to nullify a judgment. However, it has been a historical prerogative of the executive to use his authority to settle disputes between U.S. nationals and foreign states, even where the resolution was not to the liking of the U.S. nationals. Congress has never prohibited this and has enacted the 1949 International Claims Settlement Act, which created procedures for disbursing settlement amounts. From this, it can be inferred that Congress has implicitly authorized presidential action in this area. This being the case, the president had the power to act as he did. Affirmed.

▶ ANALYSIS

Whenever presidential power is analyzed, the chief authority is usually *Youngstown Sheet & Tube Co. v. Sawyer*, 343 U.S. 579 (1952). Justice Jackson's concurrence is the most oft-quoted portion of the opinion. The concept of presidential power encompassing a spectrum from congressional authorization to congressional opposition was most clearly articulated there.

Quicknotes

ARBITRATION An agreement to have a dispute heard and decided by a neutral third party, rather than through legal proceedings.

EXECUTIVE ORDER An order issued by the President, or another executive of government, which has the force of law.

Breard v. Greene, The Republic of Paraguay v. Gilmore

Convicted murderer (D) v. State (P)

523 U.S. 371 (1998).

NATURE OF CASE: Appeal from denial of habeas corpus.

FACT SUMMARY: [Breard (D), a Paraguayan citizen, claimed that his conviction should be overturned because of alleged violations of the Vienna Convention on Consular Relations—but had failed to raise this claim before his federal habeas proceedings.]

RULE OF LAW
When a statute that is subsequent in time is inconsistent with a treaty, the statute to the extent of conflict renders the treaty null.

FACTS: [Breard (D), a Paraguayan citizen, was scheduled to be executed following his conviction for murder. Breard (D) filed for habeas relief in federal court, arguing that the arresting authorities had wrongfully failed to inform him that, as a foreign national, he had the right to contact the Paraguayan consulate (D) under the Vienna Convention on Consular Relations (Convention). However, he had failed to raise this Convention claim in the state proceedings, and only raised it in his federal habeas proceedings. The State (P) contended that the claim was precluded by the procedural default doctrine; Breard (D) contended that the Convention trumped the doctrine.]

ISSUE: When a statute that is subsequent in time is inconsistent with a treaty, does the statute render the treaty null?

HOLDING AND DECISION: (Per curiam) Yes. When a statute that is subsequent in time is inconsistent with a treaty, the statute to the extent of conflict renders the treaty null. It is clear that Breard (D) procedurally-defaulted his claim. The argument that the Convention trumps the procedural default doctrine, because the Convention is the "supreme law of the land," is incorrect for two reasons. First, the procedural rules of a forum state govern the implementation of a treaty in that state. It is the rule in the United States, and in its states, that in criminal-proceeding a claim of error that is not raised by the defense in state court may not be raised on habeas. Therefore, Breard (D) failed to exercise his rights under the Convention in conformity with the laws of the United States and its states. Second, Breard's (D) argument that the Vienna Convention was violated must fail because Congress enacted the Antiterrorism and Effective Death Penalty Act after the Vienna Convention. The executive branch has authority over foreign relations and may utilize diplomatic channels to request a stay of execution. Petition denied.

ANALYSIS

The Court also held that the Eleventh Amendment barred suits against states. The Consul General of Paraguay tried to raise a §1983 suit. The Court found that Paraguay was not authorized to do so.

Quicknotes

42 U.S.C. §1983 Provides that every person, who under color of state law subjects or causes to be subjected any citizen of the United States or person within its jurisdiction to be deprived of rights, privileges and immunities guaranteed by the federal constitution and laws, is liable to the injured party at law or in equity.

ELEVENTH AMENDMENT The Eleventh Amendment to the United States Constitution prohibiting the extension of the judicial powers of the federal courts to suits brought against a state by citizens of another state, or of a foreign state, without the state's consent.

HABEAS CORPUS A proceeding in which a defendant brings a writ to compel a judicial determination of whether he is lawfully being held in custody.

Case Concerning Avena and Other Mexican Nationals (Mexico v. United States of America)

Mexican nationals (P) v. United States (D)

2004 I.C.J. 1 (Mar. 31).

NATURE OF CASE: International Court of Justice consideration of remedies available to individuals when state violates Vienna Convention.

FACT SUMMARY: United States (D) breached its obligation under Article 36(1)(b) of the Vienna Convention (Convention) to inform 51 detained Mexican nationals (P) of their rights under the Convention and to notify the Mexican consular of their detention and to allow the consular access to the detained nationals, and the nationals sought remedies for the breach in U.S. courts.

🏛 RULE OF LAW

The procedural default rule does not preclude judicial review in United States courts of cases in which the United States has breached the Vienna Convention.

FACTS: United States (D) breached its obligation under Article 36(1)(b) of the Vienna Convention (Convention) to inform 51 detained Mexican nationals (P) of their rights under the Convention and to notify the Mexican consular of their detention and to allow the consular access to the detained nationals. Under U.S. criminal procedure, foreign nationals who do not raise their Article 36 claims at trial may not raise that claim on appeal, however meritorious. Mexico (P) argued that partial or total overturning of the conviction or sentence is the necessary and sole remedy for the U.S. breach. The United States (D) argued that clemency officials are not bound by the principles of procedural default or other limitations on judicial review.

ISSUE: Does the procedural default rule preclude judicial review in United States courts of cases in which the United States has breached the Vienna Convention?

HOLDING AND DECISION: [Judge not stated in casebook excerpt.] No. The procedural default rule does not preclude judicial review in United States courts of cases in which the United States (D) has breached the Vienna Convention. Partial or total overturning of the convictions is not an available remedy here, because it is not the conviction or sentences of the Mexican nationals (P) that violate international law. Rather, it is the U.S. (D) violation of the Vienna Convention. Examination of the possible prejudice to the nationals (P) that resulted from the U.S. (D) breach of the Vienna Convention can be achieved through review of the record by a court.

▶ ANALYSIS

Clemency officials are typically members of the executive branch of government. The United States argued in this case, essentially, that the proper forum for review of claims under the Vienna Convention is the executive branch, not the judicial branch.

■═■

Sanchez-Llamas v. Oregon

Foreign national (P) v. State (D)

548 U.S. 231 (2006).

NATURE OF CASE: [The procedural posture of the case is not indicated in the casebook extract.]

FACT SUMMARY: [Foreign nationals (P) claimed on habeas that they were deprived of their rights under the Vienna Convention on Consular Relations, but did not raise their claims at trial or on direct appeal.]

RULE OF LAW

The rule of procedural default applies to the Vienna Convention on Consular Relations.

FACTS: [Two foreign nationals, Sanchez-Llamas (P) and Bustillo (P), were arrested in the United States but not advised of their rights under the Vienna Convention. Neither was sentenced to death. Bustillo's (P) efforts to raise Vienna Convention claims on habeas were denied on the ground that he failed to raise them at trial or on direct appeal. Before the Supreme Court, Bustillo (P) argued that application of the procedural default rule was inconsistent with his Vienna Convention rights.]

ISSUE: Does the rule of procedural default apply to the Vienna Convention on Consular Relations?

HOLDING AND DECISION: [Judge not stated in the casebook excerpt.] Yes. The rule of procedural default applies to the Vienna Convention on Consular Relations. Decisions by the International Court of Justice (ICJ) to the contrary, while deserving of respectful consideration, do not require the Court to change its prior understanding of the Convention. Under Article III of the Constitution, the judicial power of the United States is vested in the Supreme Court and extends to treaties. Determination of the meaning of treaties as a matter of federal law is therefore the province of the Supreme Court, which gives great weight to the opinions of those governmental departments that negotiate and enforce treaties. In this instance, the United States is not of the view that the ICJ's interpretation of the Convention's Article 36 is binding on U.S. courts. Therefore, the ICJ's decisions are entitled only to respectful consideration. Even when accorded such consideration, however, the ICJ's interpretations cannot overcome the plain import of Article 36. As held in past precedents, the procedural rules of domestic law generally govern the implementation of an international treaty. Thus, in the United States the rule of procedural default—which applies even to claimed violations of the Constitution—applies to Vienna Convention claims. [As to the argument that a violation of the Vienna Convention requires the suppression of incriminating statements made to the police after a foreign national's arrest, where a treaty does not provide a particular remedy, it is not for the federal courts to impose one on the states through law-making of their own.]

▶ *ANALYSIS*

This case involved foreign nationals who were arrested but not advised of their Convention rights. One of the issues before the Court was whether Article 36 of the Vienna Convention grants rights that may be invoked by individuals in a judicial proceeding. In reaching the other issues presented, the Court assumed, without deciding the issue, that the Vienna Convention grants such rights to individuals. However, strong arguments were made that there is a presumption that a treaty will be enforced through political and diplomatic channels, rather than through the courts. Thus, it is still undetermined whether in the U.S. Article 36 grants arrested foreign nationals a judicially enforceable right to request that their consular officers be notified of their detention, and an accompanying right to be informed by authorities of the availability of consular notification.

Medellín v. Texas

Mexican national (D) v. State (P)

552 U.S. 491 (2008).

NATURE OF CASE: Appeal of death sentence.

FACT SUMMARY: After Texas (P) convicted José Medellín (D), he appealed on the grounds that Texas (P) failed to inform him of his right to have consular personnel notified of his detention by the state, as required under the Vienna Convention. On appeal to the United States Supreme Court, Medellín (D) argued that a case decided by the International Court of Justice suggested that his conviction must be reconsidered to comply with the Vienna Convention.

🏛 RULE OF LAW
(1) The U.S. Constitution does not require state courts to honor a treaty obligation of the United States by enforcing a decision of the International Court of Justice.
(2) The U.S. Constitution does not require state courts to provide review and reconsideration of a conviction without regard to state procedural default rules as required by a Memorandum by the President.

FACTS: José Medellín (D), a Mexican national, was convicted and sentenced. In his appeal, Medellín (D) argued that the state had violated his rights under the Vienna Convention, to which the United States is a party. Article 36 of the Vienna Convention gives any foreign national detained for a crime the right to contact his consulate. The United States Supreme Court dismissed the petition and Medellín's (D) case was remanded to the Texas Court of Criminal Appeals, which also denied him relief. The United States Supreme Court took up his case again, and Medellín's (D) argument rested in part on a holding by the International Court of Justice (ICJ.) in *Case Concerning Avena and Other Mexican Nationals (Mex. v. U.S.)*, 2004 I. C.J. 12, that the United States had violated the Vienna Convention rights of 51 Mexican nationals (including Medellín (D)) and that their state-court convictions must be reconsidered, regardless of any forfeiture of the right to raise the Vienna Convention claims because of a failure to follow state rules governing criminal convictions. Medellín (D) argued that the Vienna Convention granted him an individual right that state courts must respect. Medellín (D) also cited a memorandum from the U.S. President that instructed state courts to comply with the ICJ's rulings by rehearing the cases. Medellín (D) argued that the Constitution gives the President broad power to ensure that treaties are enforced, and that this power extends to the treatment of treaties in state court proceedings.

ISSUE:
(1) Does the U.S. Constitution require state courts to honor a treaty obligation of the United States by enforcing a decision of the International Court of Justice?
(2) Does the U.S. Constitution require state courts to provide review and reconsideration of a conviction without regard to state procedural default rules as required by a Memorandum by the President?

HOLDING AND DECISION: (Roberts, C.J.)
(1) No. The U.S. Constitution does not require state courts to honor a treaty obligation of the United States by enforcing a decision of the International Court of Justice. The Vienna Convention provides that if a person detained by a foreign country asks, the authorities of the detaining national must, without delay, inform the consular post of the detainee of the detention. The Optional Protocol of the Convention provides that the International Court of Justice is the venue for resolution of issues of interpretation of the Vienna Convention. By ratifying the Optional Protocol to the Vienna Convention, the United States consented to the jurisdiction of the ICJ with respect to claims arising out of the Vienna Convention. In 2005, however, after *Avena* was decided, the United States gave notice of withdrawal from the Optional Protocol. While *Avena* constitutes an international law obligation on the part of the United States, it does not help Medellín (D) because not all international law obligations automatically constitute binding federal law. *Avena* does not have automatic domestic legal effect such that the judgment if its own force applies in state and federal courts, because it is not a self-executing treaty and Congress did not enact legislation implementing binding effect. Thus, the ICJ judgment is not automatically enforceable domestic law, immediately and directly binding on state and federal courts under the Supremacy Clause.
(2) No. The U.S. Constitution does not require state courts to provide review and reconsideration of a conviction without regard to state procedural default rules as required by a Memorandum by the President. The Presidential Memorandum was an attempt by the executive branch to enforce a non-self-executing treaty without the necessary congressional action, giving it no binding authority on state courts.

CONCURRENCE: (Stevens, J.) Although the judgment is correct, Texas (P) ought to comply with *Avena*.

Continued on next page.

Avena may not be the supreme law of the land, but it constitutes an international law obligation on the part of the United States. Since Texas (P) failed to provide consular notice in accordance with the Vienna Convention, thereby getting the United States into this mess, and since that violation probably didn't prejudice Medellín (D), Texas (P) ought to comply with *Avena*.

DISSENT: (Breyer, J.) The majority does not point to a single ratified U.S. treaty that contains the self-executing language it says is required in this case. The absence or presence of language in a treaty about a provision's self-execution proves nothing. The relevant treaty provisions should be found to be self-executing, because (1) the language supports direct judicial enforceability, (2) the Optional Protocol applies to disputes about the meaning of a provision that is itself self-executing and judicially enforceable, (3) logic requires a conclusion that the provision is self-executing since it is "final" and "binding," (4) the majority's decision has negative practical implications, (5) the ICJ judgment is well suited to direct judicial enforcement, (6) such a holding would not threaten constitutional conflict with other branches, and (7) neither the President nor Congress has expressed concern about direct judicial enforcement of the ICJ decision.

▶ *ANALYSIS*

Medellín (D) was executed on August 5, 2008, after last-minute appeals to the United States Supreme Court were rejected. Governor Rick Perry rejected calls from Mexico and Secretary of State Condoleezza Rice and Attorney General Michael Mukasey to delay the execution, citing the torture, rape, and strangulation of two teenage girls in Houston as just cause for the death penalty. Though a bill was introduced in the House of Representatives to respond to the Court's ruling, Congress took no action.

■■■

Filartiga v. Pena-Irala

Relative of decedent (P) v. Police officer (D)

630 F.2d 876 (2d Cir. 1980).

NATURE OF CASE: Appeal of dismissal of action for wrongful death.

FACT SUMMARY: The Filartigas (P) sued Pena-Irala (Pena) (D) for damages which occurred as a result of the wrongful death of their family member. Pena (D), a Paraguayan citizen, argued that the United States did not have jurisdiction to the claim.

> 🏛 **RULE OF LAW**
> Torture is considered a violation of international law, and federal jurisdiction for an action based on torture may be founded on personal jurisdiction, no matter where the tort occurred.

FACTS: Joel Filartiga (father) (P), Dolly Filartiga (daughter) (P), and Pena-Irala (Pena) (D) were Paraguayan citizens. The Filartigas (P) brought an action against Pena (D) for damages for wrongfully causing the death of their seventeen-year-old son and brother, respectively, Joelito. Joel Filartiga (P) was a long-standing opponent of the government of the President of Paraguay. The Filartigas' (P) claim that Joelito was tortured and killed by Pena (D), who was the Inspector General of Police in Paraguay, because of Joel Fiartiga's (P) beliefs. When Pena (D) entered the United States on a visitor's visa, Dolly Filartiga (P) had a summons and complaint, which invoked the Alien Torture Statute (ATS), served on him. The ATS provides that the district courts shall have original jurisdiction of any civil action by an alien for a tort only if committed in violation of the law of nations. The complaint was dismissed on jurisdictional grounds and the Filartigas' (P) appealed.

ISSUE: Does the alleged conduct violate the law of nations and thus fall under ATS, and, if it does, does federal jurisdiction to hear the claim exist?

HOLDING AND DECISION: (Kaufman, J.) Yes. The alleged conduct violates the law of nations and thus falls under ATS, and federal jurisdiction to hear the claim exists. Official torture is prohibited by the law of nations, which makes no distinction between the treatment of aliens and citizens. Federal jurisdiction for an action for wrongful death based on torture exists if personal jurisdiction exists no matter where the tort occurred. A state's treatment of its own citizens is a matter of international concern and the United Nations promotes human rights and fundamental freedoms for all. The right to be free from torture is a human right and a fundamental freedom guaranteed by international law via the United Nations Charter. The 1975 General Assembly Declaration on the Protection of All Persons from Being Subjected to Torture prohibits any state from permitting torture. Moreover, the international consensus surrounding torture has found expression in numerous international treaties and accords. In addition, torture is prohibited by Paraguay's own constitution. International law thus confers fundamental rights upon all people vis-à-vis their own governments. Furthermore, Congress provided in the Judiciary Act federal jurisdiction over suits by aliens where principles of international law are in issue. The constitutional basis for ATS is the law of nations, which has always been part of the federal common law. A case properly arises under the law of the United States for Article III purposes if grounded upon statutes enacted by Congress or upon the common law of the United States. Reversed.

▌ ANALYSIS

This opinion confirms the belief that it is every nation's responsibility to be the enforcer of international law.

■▭■

Sosa v. Alvarez-Machain

Kidnapper (D) v. Alleged foreign torturer (P)

542 U.S. 692 (2004).

NATURE OF CASE: Appeal of judgment awarding damages to foreign national.

FACT SUMMARY: [An alleged Mexican torturer brought suit for damages against the United States and the individual who abducted him and brought him to the United States for trial.]

RULE OF LAW
The Alien Tort Statute (ATS) does not create a cause of action for individuals who are victims of international law violations.

FACTS: [Enrique Camarena-Salazar was an agent of the Drug Enforcement Administration (DEA), and was captured while on assignment in Mexico. He was tortured over two days, and then murdered. Humberto Alvarez-Machain (Alvarez) (P), a Mexican physician, acted to prolong Camarena-Salazar's life in order to extend the interrogation and torture. A U.S. federal grand jury indicted Alvarez (P) for the torture and murder, and a federal district court issued a warrant for his arrest. The Mexican government would not help get Alvarez (P) to the United States, so the DEA hired Jose Francisco Sosa (D) to abduct him. Once in American custody, Alvarez (P) moved to dismiss the indictment on grounds that his seizure violated the extradition treaty between the United States and Mexico. The district court agreed and the Ninth Circuit affirmed. The Supreme Court reversed, holding that Alvarez's (P) forcible seizure did not affect the jurisdiction of the federal court. The case was tried, and at its end the district court granted Alvarez's (P) motion for acquittal. Alvarez (P) went back to Mexico and filed a claim seeking damages from the United States under the Federal Torts Claim Act (FTCA), alleging false arrest, and from Sosa (D) under the ATS, for violation of the law of nations. The district court dismissed the claim against the United States, but awarded summary judgment and $25,000 in damages to Alvarez (P) on the ATS claim against Sosa (D). The Ninth Circuit affirmed the ATS judgment, but reversed the dismissal of the FTCA claim, on grounds that the DEA had no authority to abduct Alvarez (P). The United States Supreme Court granted certiorari.]

ISSUE: Does the ATS create a cause of action for individuals who are victims of international law violations?

HOLDING AND DECISION: (Souter, J.) No. The ATS does not create a cause of action for individuals who are victims of violation of international law. The statute was intended to be exclusively concerned with jurisdiction, in the sense of addressing the power of courts to entertain cases concerned with a certain subject. The common law indicates that the ATS conferred jurisdiction for a relatively modest set of cases, alleging violations of the traditional law of nations, including only offenses against ambassadors, violations of safe conduct, and individual actions arising out of prize captures and piracy. There is no record of congressional discussion about private actions that might be subject to ATS's jurisdictional provision, or about any need for further legislation to create private remedies. While no legal development has categorically precluded federal courts from recognizing a claim under international law as an element of common law, the discretion accorded federal courts in fashioning such claims should be restrained. Therefore, courts should require any claim based on present day international law to rest on a norm of international character accepted by the civilized world and defined with specificity. Reversed.

CONCURRENCE: (Scalia, J.) While the holding that the ATS is a jurisdictional statute creating no new causes of action is correct, federal courts do not enjoy any level of discretion in considering new causes of action. While it is true that no development between the enactment of the ATS in 1789 and the birth of modern international human rights litigation under that statute in 1980 has precluded federal courts from recognizing a claim under international law, the proper question is not whether any case or congressional action prevents federal courts from applying the law of nations as part of the general common law, but what authorizes that exception from fundamental precedent holding that a general common law does not exist?

ANALYSIS

The events giving rise to this case are 20 years old. This was the first and last time the Supreme Court addressed the scope of the ATS. According to this decision, then, federal courts might still recognize an individual cause of action under the ATS.

Khulumani v. Barclay National Bank

Apartheid victims' representative (P) v. Multinational corporation (D)

504 F.3d 254 (2d Cir. 2007).

NATURE OF CASE: Appeal from dismissal of action brought under the Alien Tort Statute, 28 U.S.C. §1350.

FACT SUMMARY: [Representatives (P) of apartheid victims in South Africa claimed that various multinational corporations (D) aided and abetted the apartheid government in various ways.]

> 🏛 **RULE OF LAW**
> Aiding and abetting violations of customary international law can provide a basis for jurisdiction under the Alien Tort Statute (ATS), 28 U.S.C. §1350.

FACTS: [Representatives (P) of apartheid victims in South Africa sued various multinational corporations (D), alleging violations of international law, as well as claims under, inter alia, the ATS. The victims' representatives (P) alleged, inter alia, that the corporations (D), which had manufacturing operations in South Africa or supported such operations, aided and abetted South Africa's apartheid government's human rights violations in various ways. The district court granted the corporations' (D) motion to dismiss, holding that aiding and abetting violations of customary international law cannot provide a basis for ATS jurisdiction. The court of appeals granted review.]

ISSUE: Can aiding and abetting violations of customary international law provide a basis for jurisdiction under the ATS, 28 U.S.C. §1350?

HOLDING AND DECISION: [Judge not stated in casebook excerpt.] Yes. Aiding and abetting violations of customary international law can provide a basis for jurisdiction under the ATS, 28 U.S.C. §1350.

CONCURRENCE: (Katzmann, J.) Jurisdiction under the ATS depends on whether international law specifically recognizes liability for aiding and abetting violations of the law of nations, and this rule is consistent with Supreme Court precedent. Once the court determines that alleged conduct falls within one of the small number of international law violations with a potential for personal liability for a non-state actor, the court should consider whether United States federal common law would provide a cause of action to enable the plaintiffs to bring their claim. The recognition of the individual responsibility of a defendant who aids and abets a violation of international law is part of customary international law, and has been applied in war crimes tribunals (e.g., Military Tribunal at Nuremberg after World War II) and in various international instruments. These instruments include major agreements addressing fundamental human rights concerns such as torture, apartheid, slavery,

and genocide, as well as drug trafficking, organized crime, and more. Moreover, the term "accomplice" in such instruments has been understood to reach those who aid and abet violations of international law or international treaties. Aiding and abetting liability continues to be recognized and enforced in international tribunals, whose charters essentially codify norms of customary international law. More recently, the Rome Statute of the International Criminal Court (Rome Statute) expressly provides for the crime of aiding and abetting and sets forth the necessary mens rea for such a crime. For these reasons, a defendant may be held liable under international law for aiding and abetting the violation of that law by another when the defendant (1) provides practical assistance to the principal which has a substantial effect on the perpetration of the crime, and (2) does so with the purpose of facilitating the commission of that crime. In sum, aiding and abetting liability imposed in accordance with this standard is sufficiently well-established and universally recognized under international law to trigger jurisdiction under the ATS.

CONCURRENCE: (Hall, J.) While a federal court must turn to international law to divine standards of primary liability under the ATS, to derive a standard of aiding and abetting liability, however, the court should consult the federal common law. The ATS itself is silent on whether one can be liable for aiding and abetting a violation thereunder. Such a gap should be filled by looking to federal common law, which already provides a standard for accessorial liability and is reflected in the Restatement (Second) of Torts §876. Numerous courts have relied on this Restatement standard, and, applying this standard to ATS aiding and abetting claims, liability should be found only where there is evidence that a defendant furthered the violation of a clearly established international law norm in one of three ways: (1) by knowingly and substantially assisting a principal tortfeasor, such as a foreign government or its proxy, to commit an act that violates a clearly established international law norm; (2) by encouraging, advising, contracting with, or otherwise soliciting a principal tortfeasor to commit an act while having actual or constructive knowledge that the principal tortfeasor will violate a clearly established customary international law norm in the process of completing that act; or (3) by facilitating the commission of human rights violations by providing the principal tortfeasor with the tools, instrumentalities, or services to commit those violations with actual or constructive knowledge that those tools, instrumentalities, or services will be (or only could be) used in connection with that purpose.

Continued on next page.

▶ *ANALYSIS*

This decision should prompt officers and directors of multinational corporations to address whether their corporations are in compliance with ATS mandates, because if they are not, they could potentially face ATS actions with significant liability exposure and legal expenses—not to mention negative publicity and bruised reputations. This is especially true since the increased presence of multinational firms in all parts of the world has coincided with the increased human rights obligations and expectations of not only governments but also corporations.

■▬■

Quicknotes

AIDING AND ABETTING   Assistance given in order to facilitate the commission of a criminal act.

INTER ALIA   Among other things.

JURISDICTION   The authority of a court to hear and declare judgment in respect to a particular matter.

MENS REA   Criminal intent.

■▬■

Banco Nacional de Cuba v. Sabbatino

Cuban government (P) v. Receiver (D)

376 U.S. 398 (1964).

NATURE OF CASE: Review of order dismissing action for damages for breach of contract.

FACT SUMMARY: Faced with a breach of contract action by the Cuban government (P), Sabbatino (D) contended that an earlier expropriation of property, not protected by the act of state doctrine, constituted an offset.

🏛 RULE OF LAW
The act of state doctrine is available to a foreign government plaintiff which has expropriated property of the party it sues.

FACTS: In 1960, the Castro government of Cuba (P) nationalized certain U.S.-owned companies. One such company was Compania Azucarera, a sugar distributer. Azucarera had contracted to sell sugar to Farr, Whitlock & Co. After the sugar was nationalized, Farr, Whitlock entered into another contract, this time with the Cuban government (P). The sugar was delivered, but Farr, Whitlock refused to pay the Cuban government (P), but rather turned the proceeds over to Sabbatino (D), a receiver appointed for Azucarera's assets. The Cuban government (P) brought a breach of contract action. Sabbatino (D) raised the expropriation as an offset. The district court, rejecting the Cuban government's (P) act of state defense, granted summary judgment in favor of Sabbatino (D). The court of appeals affirmed, and the United States Supreme Court granted review.

ISSUE: Is the act of state doctrine available to a foreign government plaintiff which has expropriated the property of the party it sues?

HOLDING AND DECISION: (Harlan, J.) Yes. The act of state doctrine is available to a foreign government plaintiff which has expropriated property of the party it sues. As long ago as the last century, this Court recognized that U.S. courts may not sit in judgment of the propriety of acts done by a government within its borders. This has consistently been reaffirmed ever since. However, several reasons are advanced for not applying the act of state doctrine to a foreign government plaintiff which has expropriated property of the defendant, in this case Sabbatino's (D) predecessor. The first is that the doctrine should not apply to acts violating international law. This is incorrect. The act of state doctrine does not arise from international law; traditionally, it has been a matter of comity between individual nations. No international agreements recognize it. The other argument is that the executive must approve its application in any specific case

for it to be binding on federal courts. This is a simplistic view of the role of the judiciary in this area. The judiciary's interest in rendering decisions involving foreign bodies becomes greater in matters of consensus of codification; the less consensual or codified a concept is, the more the matter should be left to political branches of government. The matter of expropriation of foreign assets by a nation is a highly controversial one, an issue hardly near consensus in the international community. Consequently, it is a matter best left for the political branches to address. An expropriation therefore should not be the subject of judgment by a U.S. court, being a nonjusticiable act of state. Here, the basis for allowing the offset was the district court's conclusion that it could adjudicate the Venezuelan government's expropriation, and this was erroneous. Reversed.

DISSENT: (White, J.) The Court has declared the application of international law beyond the competence of U.S. courts in an important category of cases. The Court is incorrect in its assertion that the act of state doctrine cannot be adjudicated by reference to international law.

▌ *ANALYSIS*

The present decision was not popular in the political branches of government, particularly Congress. Not long after the decision was rendered, Congress enacted 22 U.S.C. §2370(e)(2), a statutory overruling of the instant case. While the law has survived constitutional attack, courts tend to construe it narrowly.

■══■

Quicknotes

ACT OF STATE DOCTRINE Prohibits United States courts from investigating acts of other countries committed within their borders.

■══■

W.S. Kirkpatrick & Co. v. Environmental Tectonics Corp., International

Contractor (D) v. Competitor (P)

493 U.S. 400 (1990).

NATURE OF CASE: Review of order reversing dismissal of action for damages for violation of federal statute.

FACT SUMMARY: [A contractor brought a civil action for damages against a competitor who had obtained a government contract in Nigeria through bribery.]

> 🏛 **RULE OF LAW**
> The act of state doctrine does not apply to an action that does not require the court to declare invalid the official act of a foreign sovereign.

FACTS: [A principal of W.S. Kirkpatrick & Co. (D) was alleged to have effected certain bribes of Nigerian officials to secure a government contract, in violation of the federal Foreign Corrupt Practices Act and Nigerian law. Environmental Tectonics Corp., International (Environmental Tectonics) (P), a competitor for the contract, informed the U.S. Attorney, who filed criminal charges against the defendants, who in turn pleaded guilty to the charges. Environmental Tectonics (P) then filed a civil action seeking damages under federal law. The district court dismissed the action, holding that since the suit implicated the actions of Nigerian officials, the act of state doctrine applied. The Third Circuit reversed, relying heavily upon a State Department letter stating that judicial inquiry into the purpose behind the act of a foreign sovereign would not produce the "unique embarrassment, and the particular interference with the conduct of foreign affairs, that may result from the judicial determination that a foreign sovereign's acts are invalid." The United States Supreme Court granted certiorari.]

ISSUE: Does the act of state doctrine apply to an action that does not require the court to declare invalid the official act of a foreign sovereign?

HOLDING AND DECISION: [Judge not stated in casebook excerpt.] No. The act of state doctrine does not apply to an action that does not require the court to declare invalid the official act of a foreign sovereign. The act of state doctrine has been described as a consequence of domestic separation of powers, to wit, recognition by the judiciary that certain situations involving relations with foreign governments are a matter of concern for the executive, and judicial decisions respecting such issues could interfere with executive action in this area. Essentially it is for the executive to engage in foreign affairs and to pass on the validity of foreign acts of state. When these concerns are not implicated, the act of state doctrine is not applicable.

When a judicial decision does not pass on such validity, no reason for abstaining from otherwise proper jurisdiction exists. In this particular case, no issue exists as to the validity of any act by the Nigerian government. The issues pertain to the alleged actions by agents of W.S. Kirkpatrick (D). Since the outcome of the present case only tangentially implicates the acts of a foreign government, the act of state doctrine is inapplicable. Affirmed.

▶ ANALYSIS

Over the years, the act of state doctrine has taken on an increasingly domestic focus. As late as 1918, in *Oetjen v. Central Leather Co.*, 246 U.S. 297 (1918), the Court gave as authority for the doctrine concerns of international comity. In the present action, however, the Court makes it clear that the main focus of the doctrine is intragovernmental relations, not international relations.

■=■

Quicknotes

ACT OF STATE DOCTRINE Prohibits United States courts from investigating acts of other countries committed within their borders.

NONJUSTICIABLE Matter which is inappropriate for judicial review.

SEPARATION OF POWERS The system of checks and balances preventing one branch of government from infringing upon exercising the powers of another branch of government.

■=■

The Reach of Domestic Law in the International Arena

Quick Reference Rules of Law

CHAPTER

The S.S. "Lotus" (France/Turkey)

Nation disputing jurisdiction (P) v. Nation asserting jurisdiction (D)

Permanent Ct. Int'l Justice, P.C.I.J., Ser. A, No. 10, p. 4 (1927).

NATURE OF CASE: Action to determine validity of exercise of criminal jurisdiction.

FACT SUMMARY: [France (P) contended that Turkey (D) violated international law by asserting jurisdiction over a French citizen who had been the first officer of a ship which collided with a Turkish ship on the high seas.]

> ## 🏛 RULE OF LAW
> There is no rule of international law prohibiting a state from exercising criminal jurisdiction over a foreign national who commits acts outside of the state's national jurisdiction.

FACTS: [A collision occurred between the French (P) mail steamer Lotus, which was captained by Demons, a French citizen, and the Turkish (D) vessel Boz-Kourt, which was cut in two and sank, killing eight Turkish (D) nationals. After having done everything possible to help the shipwrecked persons, the Lotus continued on its course to Constantinople, where it arrived the next day. Two days later, Demons was requested by the Turkish (D) authorities to go ashore to give evidence. The examination led to the placing under arrest of Demons, without previous notice being given to the French (P) Consul-General, and Demons was subsequently charged with manslaughter, of which he was convicted. The Turkish (D) courts rejected Demons's argument that they lacked jurisdiction over him. France (P) and Turkey (D) then agreed to submit to the Permanent Court of International Justice the question of whether the exercise of Turkish (D) criminal jurisdiction over Demons for an incident that occurred on the high seas violated international law.]

ISSUE: Is there a rule of international law prohibiting a state from exercising criminal jurisdiction over a foreign national who commits acts outside of the state's national jurisdiction?

HOLDING AND DECISION: [Judge not stated in casebook excerpt.] No. There is no rule of international law prohibiting a state from exercising criminal jurisdiction over a foreign national who commits acts outside of the state's national jurisdiction. The first and foremost restriction imposed by international law upon a state is that, failing the existence of a permissive rule to the contrary, it may not exercise its power in any form in the territory of another state. It does not, however, follow that international law prohibits a state from exercising jurisdiction in its own territory, in respect of any case which relates to acts which have taken place abroad, and in which it cannot rely on some permissive rule of international law. The territoriality of criminal law is not an absolute principle of international law, and by no means coincides with territorial sovereignty. Here, because the effects of the alleged offense occurred on a Turkish (D) vessel, it is impossible to hold that there is a rule of international law which prohibits Turkey (D) from prosecuting Lieutenant Demons simply because he was aboard a French (P) ship at the time of the incident. Because there is no rule of international law in regard to collision cases to the effect that criminal proceedings are exclusively within the jurisdiction of the state whose flag is flown, both states here may exercise concurrent jurisdiction over this matter.

▶ ANALYSIS

In conformity with the holding of this case, France in 1975 enacted a law regarding its criminal jurisdiction over aliens. That law, cited in 102 *Journal Du Droit International* 962 (Clunet 1975), provides that aliens who commit a crime outside of the territory of the Republic may be prosecuted and judged pursuant to French law, when the victim is of French nationality. The holding in this case has been criticized by several eminent scholars for seeming to imply that international law permits all that it does not forbid.

■■■■

United States v. Aluminum Co. of America (Alcoa)

Federal government (P) v. Corporation (D)

148 F.2d 416 (2d Cir. 1945).

NATURE OF CASE: Appeal of an antitrust action against foreign companies.

FACT SUMMARY: Limited (D), a Canadian corporation, and several European aluminum companies made agreements that were accused of being in violation of U.S. antitrust law.

🏛 RULE OF LAW
Agreements made outside of the United States are unlawful under the Sherman Act (Act) if they would have been considered unlawful if made within the United States and they were intended to affect imports and did indeed affect them.

FACTS: The Alliance was a Swiss corporation created through an agreement among Limited (D) and several European companies. The Alliance made agreements in 1931 and 1936 that governed the sale of aluminum by Limited (D) and the European companies. The agreements were accused of being in violation of U.S. antitrust laws.

ISSUE: Are agreements made outside of the United States unlawful under the Sherman Act (Act) if they would have been considered unlawful if made within the United States and they were intended to affect imports and did indeed affect them?

HOLDING AND DECISION: [Judge not stated in casebook excerpt.] Yes. Agreements made outside of the United States are unlawful under the Sherman Act (Act) if they would have been considered unlawful if made within the United States and they were intended to affect imports and did indeed affect them. The agreement of 1936 violated the Sherman Act because it was intended to restrict imports into the United States (P) and, indeed, had such an effect. The concern is whether Congress chose to attach liability to the conduct of persons outside the United States (P) who are not in allegiance to it and whether our own Constitution permitted Congress to do so. Although a United States (P) court cannot look beyond its own laws, it must read its laws with regard to the limitations customarily observed by nations upon the exercise of their powers or limitations as described by the "Conflict of Laws." Congress does not intend to punish all those it can catch for conduct that has no consequence in the United States (P). However, any state may impose liabilities upon persons not within its allegiance for conduct outside its borders that has consequences within its borders that the state reprehends. Other states will ordinarily recognize these liabilities. Furthermore, the Act may also extend to agreements made beyond our borders that are not intended to affect our imports but that do affect them, or that affect exports. Congress, however, could not have intended the Act to cover those instances. The Act, therefore, does not cover agreements, even if those agreements intended to affect imports or exports, unless its performance is shown to actually have had some effect upon them. In the present case, the agreements would have been considered unlawful if made within the United States (P). Since they were made outside of the United States (P), they would be unlawful under the Act if they were intended to affect imports and did affect them. The 1936 agreement restricting production was intended to restrict imports into the United States (P). It had such an effect, and therefore was in violation of U.S. antitrust laws.

▶ ANALYSIS

This case illustrates that U.S. law will reach foreign entities if their actions are intended to affect and indeed do affect U.S. trade or commerce even though their activities primarily occur outside of the United States.

Quicknotes

ANTITRUST Body of federal law prohibiting business conduct that constitutes a restraint on trade.

SHERMAN ACT Prohibits unreasonable restraint of trade.

Timberlane Lumber Co. v. Bank of America

Lumber company (P) v. Bank (D)

549 F.2d 597 (9th Cir. 1976).

NATURE OF CASE: Appeal of dismissal, on jurisdictional grounds, of antitrust action.

FACT SUMMARY: Timberlane Lumber Co. (P) argued that the United States had jurisdiction to hear its antitrust case because Bank of America's (the bank) (D) actions had an effect on U.S. foreign commerce, but the bank (D) argued that more was needed to compel jurisdiction.]

RULE OF LAW

In determining whether U.S. courts have jurisdiction over actions involving effects on U.S. foreign commerce, courts must weigh not only the magnitude of the effects but also whether conflict-of-laws considerations warrant an assertion of extraterritorial authority.

FACTS: [Timberlane Lumber Co. (Timberlane) (P), a U.S. partnership, imported lumber from Central America into the United States. Timberlane sought to establish operations in Honduras. Bank of America (the bank) (D) financed much of the Honduran lumber industry. After a Honduran company financed by the bank (D) went bankrupt, the company's assets passed to the company's creditors, who sold the assets to Timberlane (P). After Timberlane (P) began operations in Honduras, the bank (D) allegedly conspired with Honduran lumber companies to drive Timberlane (P) out of business in order to enable other companies financed by the bank to continue to monopolize the Honduran lumber market. The district court dismissed the complaint for lack of subject matter jurisdiction and on act of state grounds. Timberlane (P) alleged that the activities at issue were intended to and did affect the export of lumber from Honduras to the United States and that the complained-of activities were therefore within the jurisdiction of the federal courts under the Sherman Act. The bank (D) argued that more analysis was needed. The court of appeals granted review.]

ISSUE: In determining whether U.S. courts have jurisdiction over actions involving effects on U.S. foreign commerce, must courts weigh not only the magnitude of the effects but also whether conflict-of-laws considerations warrant an assertion of extraterritorial authority?

HOLDING AND DECISION: (Choy, J.) Yes. In determining whether U.S. courts have jurisdiction over actions involving effects on U.S. foreign commerce, courts must weigh not only the magnitude of the effects but also whether conflict-of-laws considerations warrant an assertion of extraterritorial authority. More factors need to be considered than just the effects test. The magnitude of the effect alleged by Timberlane (P) would appear sufficient to state a claim. The comity question, however, complicates the situation since some of the defendants are foreign citizens, most of the activity took place in Honduras, and most of the economic effect was in Honduras. Also, there is no indication of any conflict with the law or policy of the Honduran government nor any comprehensive analysis of the relative connections and interests of Honduras and the United States to compel jurisdiction in the United States. Although American antitrust law extends over some conduct in other nations, it does not cover all conduct. Foreign countries have complained when U.S. courts have interfered, via their decisions, with the actions of entities within foreign borders. At some point the goal of harmony with foreign nations is stronger than U.S. interests to justify an extraterritorial assertion of jurisdiction. U.S. courts have thus considered the interests of other nations when applying the effects test. These other elements that are taken into consideration along with the effects tests demonstrate that a tripartite analysis should therefore be done. First, U.S. courts will exercise subject matter jurisdiction when there is an actual or intended effect on U.S. foreign commerce. Second, the effect must be substantially large to present an injury to the plaintiffs. Third, a determination is to be made as to whether the interests of the United States are sufficiently strong as compared to other nations to justify an assertion of extraterritorial authority. In regard to this third prong, an effect on U.S. commerce alone is not a sufficient basis to confer jurisdiction. The field of conflict of laws presents the proper approach and several elements are to be weighed. Among the elements is the degree of conflict with foreign law or policy, the allegiance of the parties and the principal place of business of the corporation, the extent to which enforcement by either state can be expected to achieve compliance, the relative significance to the United States as compared with those elsewhere, the extent to which there is an explicit purpose to harm U.S. commerce, the foreseeability of such effect and the relative importance of the violation charged within the United States as compared with conduct abroad. In light of all of these factors, the dismissal by the district court cannot be sustained on jurisdictional grounds. Reversed.

▶ *ANALYSIS*

United States v. Aluminum Co. of America (ALCOA), 148 F.2d 416 (2d Cir. 1945), focused primarily on the effects test to determine jurisdiction; this case says that there has to be more analysis done than just the effects test to confer jurisdiction on the United States.

■■■

Continued on next page.

Quicknotes

ANTITRUST Body of federal law prohibiting business conduct that constitutes a restraint on trade.

Hartford Fire Insurance Co. v. California

Foreign-based reinsurer (D) v. State (P)

509 U.S. 764 (1993).

NATURE OF CASE: Appeal from a judgment as to jurisdiction and application of domestic law to a foreign company in a federal antitrust action.

FACT SUMMARY: Claiming that Hartford Fire Insurance Co. (D) and other London-based reinsurers (D) had allegedly engaged in unlawful conspiracies to affect the market for insurance in the United States, California (P) instituted an action against Hartford (D), under the Sherman Act, which the reinsurers (D) sought to dismiss under the principle of international comity.

> **RULE OF LAW**
> Where a person subject to regulation by two states can comply with the laws of both, jurisdiction may be exercised over foreign conduct since no conflict exists.

FACTS: California (P) brought an action against Hartford Fire Insurance Co. (Hartford) (D) and other London-based reinsurers (D) alleging that they had engaged in unlawful conspiracies to affect the market for insurance in the United States and that their conduct in fact produced substantial effect, thus violating the Sherman Act. Hartford (D) argued that the district court should have declined to exercise jurisdiction under the principle of international comity. The court of appeals agreed that courts should look to that principle in deciding whether to exercise jurisdiction under the Sherman Act but that other factors, including Hartford's (D) express purpose to affect U.S. commerce and the substantial nature of the effect produced, outweighed the supposed conflict, requiring the exercise of jurisdiction in this case. Hartford (D) appealed.

ISSUE: Where a person subject to regulation by two states can comply with the laws of both, may jurisdiction be exercised over foreign conduct since no conflict exists?

HOLDING AND DECISION: (Souter, J.) Yes. Where a person subject to regulation by two states can comply with the laws of both, jurisdiction may be exercised over foreign conduct since no conflict exists. The Sherman Act applies to foreign conduct that was meant to produce and does in fact produce some substantial effect in the United States. Even assuming that a court may decline to exercise Sherman Act jurisdiction over foreign conduct, international comity would not prevent a U.S. court from exercising jurisdiction in the circumstances alleged here. Since Hartford (D) does not argue that British law requires it to act in some fashion prohibited by the law of the United States or claim that its compliance with the laws

of both countries is otherwise impossible, there is no conflict with British law. Since there is no irreconcilable conflict between domestic and British law, the reinsurers (D) may not invoke comity. Affirmed.

DISSENT: (Scalia, J.) The District Court had subject-matter jurisdiction over the Sherman Act claims, and it is now well established that the Sherman Act applies extraterritorially, despite the presumption against extraterritoriality. But, even where the presumption against extraterritoriality does not apply, statutes should not be interpreted to regulate foreign persons or conduct if that regulation would conflict with principles of international law. This concept is reflected in the Restatement (Third), which provides that a nation having some "basis" for jurisdiction to prescribe law should nonetheless refrain from exercising that jurisdiction "with respect to a person or activity having connections with another state when the exercise of such jurisdiction is unreasonable." The "reasonableness" inquiry turns on a number of factors including, but not limited to: "the extent to which the activity takes place within the territory [of the regulating state]"; "the connections, such as nationality, residence, or economic activity, between the regulating state and the person principally responsible for the activity to be regulated"; "the character of the activity to be regulated, the importance of regulation to the regulating state, the extent to which other states regulate such activities, and the degree to which the desirability of such regulation is generally accepted"; "the extent to which another state may have an interest in regulating the activity"; and "the likelihood of conflict with regulation by another state." These factors all clearly indicate that U.S. law should not apply. The activity at issue here took place primarily in the United Kingdom, and Hartford (D) and the other reinsurers (D) are British subjects having their principal place of business or residence outside the United States. Great Britain has established a comprehensive regulatory scheme governing the London reinsurance markets and clearly has a heavy interest in regulating the activity.

> ▶ **ANALYSIS**
>
> *Black's Law Dictionary* (5th ed. 1979) defines comity of nations as "[t]he recognition which one nation allows within its territory to the legislative, executive, or judicial acts of another nation, having due regard both to international duty and convenience and to the rights of its own citizens or of other persons who are under the protection

Continued on next page.

of its laws." When it enacted the Foreign Trade Antitrust Improvements Act of 1982 (FTAIA), Congress expressed no view on the question of whether a court with Sherman Act jurisdiction should ever decline to exercise such jurisdiction on grounds of international comity, an issue that the Court declined to address in this case. Justice Scalia endorsed the approach of the Restatement (Third) of Foreign Relations Law, advocating that a nation having some basis for jurisdiction should nonetheless refrain from exercising that jurisdiction when the exercise of such jurisdiction is unreasonable.

■■■

Quicknotes

ANTITRUST LAW Body of federal law prohibiting business conduct that constitutes a restraint on trade.

COMITY A rule pursuant to which courts in one state give deference to the statutes and judicial decisions of another.

■■■

Re Wood Pulp Cartel

European Community (P) v. Wood pulp producers/exporters (D)

[1988] E.C.R. 5193.

NATURE OF CASE: Appeal to the European Court of Justice from a decision extending jurisdiction beyond the European Community's (EC) territory for extraterritorial anticompetitive conduct that impacts the EC.

FACT SUMMARY: Producers of wood pulp and trade associations outside the EC engaged in practices that had an anticompetitive impact on wood pulp prices within the EC. The European Commission asserted extraterritorial jurisdiction.

🏛 RULE OF LAW
The European Community has extraterritorial jurisdiction over parties whose anticompetitive conduct is implemented within the Community.

FACTS: Producers of wood pulp and trade associations (D) outside the EC engaged in practices that had an anticompetitive impact on wood pulp prices within the EC (60 percent of total consumption of wood pulp was affected). These defendants either exported directly to EC purchasers, or did business in the EC through branches, subsidiaries, agents, or other EC establishments. The European Commission asserted extraterritorial jurisdiction over the producers and associations, who appealed. The European Court of Justice granted review.

ISSUE: Does the European Community have extraterritorial jurisdiction over parties whose anticompetitive conduct is implemented within the Community?

HOLDING AND DECISION: [Judge not stated in casebook excerpt.] Yes. The European Community has extraterritorial jurisdiction over parties whose anticompetitive conduct is implemented within the Community. Assertion of extraterritorial jurisdiction over the wood pulp producers and trade associations (D) is not incompatible with public international law on the ground that such conduct occurred outside the EC. An infringement of Article 85 of the Treaty of Rome, prohibiting anticompetitive conduct, had two elements: (1) the formation of the agreement or practice, and (2) the implementation thereof. If the applicability of Article 85 was limited to the place where the anticompetitive conduct was formed, it would be easy to evade its prohibitions. Therefore, the place where the conduct is implemented is decisive of jurisdiction. Here, the pricing agreements were implemented in the EC, and, accordingly, the EC's jurisdiction to apply its competition rules to such conduct is covered by the territoriality principle universally recognized in international law. Members of KEA [a U.S.-based export association] claim that the EC should not exercise jurisdiction on the basis of the principle of noninterference—where if two states have jurisdiction to enforce rules that if enforced by each state would subject a person to contradictory orders of conduct, each state is obliged to exercise its jurisdiction with moderation. Here, however, there is no contradiction between U.S. antitrust laws and the EC's competition rules.

▶ ANALYSIS

Although the EC and other governments have protested the assertion of extraterritorial jurisdiction by the United States under it antitrust laws, they continue to interpret their own antitrust laws to permit jurisdiction over foreign conduct. They maintain that the EC's implementation test, as set forth in the *Wood Pulp* case, is not the same as the effects test used by U.S. courts, which is also used to justify extraterritorial jurisdiction.

■=■

Quicknotes

ANTITRUST Body of federal law prohibiting business conduct that constitutes a restraint on trade.

■=■

Attorney-General of the State of Israel v. Adolf Eichmann

State (P) v. Convicted criminal (D)

36 I.L.R. 277 (1962).

NATURE OF CASE: Appeal of conviction and death sentence.

FACT SUMMARY: Eichmann (D) was convicted and sentenced to death for crimes against humanity. He (D) appealed and argued that the State of Israel (P) did not have jurisdiction to try him.

🏛 RULE OF LAW
When the crimes attributed to a defendant are of an international character and are so evil and murderous as to shake the very foundation of the international community, a state has jurisdiction to try the offender based on the principle of universality, notwithstanding that the crimes did not occur in that state or that the offender is not a citizen of that state.

FACTS: Eichmann (D) was found guilty by the District Court of Jerusalem of extremely grave offenses during World War II and was sentenced to death. He (D) appealed, arguing that Israel (P) did not have jurisdiction to try him (D). International law holds that the offenses for which he (D) was convicted were committed outside the territory of Israel (P) by a citizen of a foreign state. Although, jurisdiction is conferred upon Israel (P) in the case of such offenses, it conflicts with the principal of territorial sovereignty which holds that only the country within whose territory the offense was committed, or to which the offender belongs, in this case Germany, has jurisdiction to punish.

ISSUE: When the crimes attributed to a defendant are of an international character and are so evil and murderous as to shake the very foundation of the international community, does a state have jurisdiction to try the offender based on the principle of universality, notwithstanding that the crimes did not occur in that state or that the offender is not a citizen of that state?

HOLDING AND DECISION: [Judge not stated in casebook excerpt.] Yes. When the crimes attributed to a defendant are of an international character and are so evil and murderous as to shake the very foundation of the international community, a state has jurisdiction to try the offender based on the principle of universality, notwithstanding that the crimes did not occur in that state or that the offender is not a citizen of that state. Based on the principle of universality, the District Court of Jerusalem had jurisdiction to try Eichmann (D). It is the universal character of the crimes which vests in every state the power to try those who participated in the perpetration of such crimes and to punish them, even though the offense was committed outside of the trying country's territory by a person who was not a citizen of the country, provided he is in custody when he is brought to trial. In such instances, the state is acting as a guardian and enforcer of international law. Although there are various schools of thought in regard to the scope of the application of universality, there is full justification for applying in this case the principle of universal jurisdiction because the international character of the crimes against humanity at issue are not in doubt and the unprecedented extent of the injurious and murderous effects is not open to dispute. Furthermore, universal jurisdiction can be exercised because most states must first offer the accused's extradition to the state in which the offense was committed, and then only if the second state does not respond to the offer of extradition may the first state claim the jurisdiction to try and punish. Because Germany refused Eichmann's (D) own demand for extradition and most of the witnesses and evidence were in Israel (P) and not in Germany, Israel can claim jurisdiction. Affirmed.

▶ ANALYSIS

The principle of universality had wide support at the time of this opinion and was universally acknowledged.

■≡■

Quicknotes

EXTRADITION The surrender by one state or nation to another of an individual allegedly guilty of committing a crime in that area.

■≡■

United States v. Yousef

Federal government (P) v. Convicted terrorist (D)

327 F.3d 56 (2d Cir. 2003).

NATURE OF CASE: Appeal of criminal conviction.

FACT SUMMARY: [Yousef (D) was charged and indicted in the United States with the bombing of a Philippines Airlines flight. He contended that the United States (P) did not have jurisdiction because there were no contacts with the United States, but the district court held that the principle of universal jurisdiction was applicable, because Yousef's (D) conduct qualified as a "terrorist" act.]

🏛 RULE OF LAW
Universal jurisdiction arises under customary international law only where crimes (1) are universally condemned by the community of nations, and (2) by their nature occur either outside of a state or where there is no state capable of punishing, or competent to punish, the crime.

FACTS: [Yousef (D) was charged in the United States, inter alia, with the bombing of a Philippines Airlines flight. He was indicted under the Aircraft Sabotage Act of 1984, which criminalizes certain offenses committed against non U.S.-flag aircraft. Yousef (D) contended that because the airplane was not a U.S.-flag aircraft, the plane was flying between two destinations outside the United States, and there was no evidence that any U.S. citizens were on the flight or targets of the bombing, the extraterritorial application of U.S. criminal statutes in these circumstances was inconsistent with international law principles regarding jurisdiction to prescribe. The district court held that the principle of universal jurisdiction was applicable because Yousef's (D) conduct qualified as a "terrorist" act. The court of appeals granted review.]

ISSUE: Does universal jurisdiction arise under customary international law only where crimes (1) are universally condemned by the community of nations, and (2) by their nature occur either outside of a state or where there is no state capable of punishing, or competent to punish, the crime?

HOLDING AND DECISION: [Judge not stated in casebook excerpt.] Yes. Universal jurisdiction arises under customary international law only where crimes (1) are universally condemned by the community of nations, and (2) by their nature occur either outside of a state or where there is no state capable of punishing, or competent to punish, the crime. Universal jurisdiction is historically restricted to piracy, war crimes, and crimes against humanity, and unlike those offenses, "terrorism" does not have a precise definition and has not achieved universal condemnation.

▶ ANALYSIS

One of the biggest impediments to defining "terrorism" is state-sponsored terrorism, or acts of state employed to effect coercion. The terrorism that is commonly understood in the United States is not similarly defined in many parts of the world. Whenever the acts of terrorism are a case's focus—whether one involving universal jurisdiction or another issue—courts will be hesitant to impose a definition.

Quicknotes

INDICTMENT A formal written accusation made by a prosecutor and issued by a grand jury, charging an individual with a criminal offense.

INTERNATIONAL LAW The body of law applicable to dealings between nations.

JURISDICTION The authority of a court to hear and declare judgment in respect to a particular matter.

Attorney-General of the Government of Israel v. Eichmann

State (P) v. Citizen of foreign country (D)

36 I.L.R. 5 (1961).

NATURE OF CASE: War crimes trial.

FACT SUMMARY: Eichmann (D) was brought from Argentina to Israel (P) to stand trial for crimes against humanity. He (D) argued that he (D) was kidnapped by agents of the State of Israel (P) and forcibly brought to Israel (P) in violation of international law and therefore Israel (P) did not have jurisdiction over him (D).

🏛 RULE OF LAW
An individual cannot assert a violation of a country's sovereignty as a basis for denying another country's jurisdiction over him.

FACTS: Eichmann (D) was accused of war crimes in a court in the State of Israel (P). He (D) argued that because he (D) was kidnapped from Argentina by agents of the State of Israel (P) and brought to Israel (P) to be arraigned on the charges, Argentina's sovereignty was violated and, therefore, Israel (P) did not have jurisdiction over him (D). The Attorney-General (P) argued that it was the duty of the Court to simply try the crimes and the Court was not to enter into the circumstances of the arrest of the accused (D) and of his (D) transfer to the area of jurisdiction of the State because these questions had no bearing on the jurisdiction of the Court to try the accused (D) for the offenses for which he (D) was being prosecuted, but only on the foreign relations between the countries. Moreover, Argentina had already resolved with Israel (P) the issue of a violation of Argentina's sovereignty as a result of the kidnapping and the issue was therefore moot.

ISSUE: Can an individual assert a violation of a country's sovereignty as a basis for denying another country's jurisdiction over him?

HOLDING AND DECISION: [Judge not stated in casebook excerpt.] No. An individual cannot assert a violation of a country's sovereignty as a basis for denying another country's jurisdiction over him. Eichmann (D) cannot plead a violation of the sovereignty of Argentina because that is a right reserved alone for Argentina to make or waive and Argentina had already resolved the issue with Israel (P). It is an established rule of law that a person being tried for an offense against the laws of a state may not oppose his trial by reason of the illegality of his arrest or the means by which he was brought within the jurisdiction of that state. Only a country can plea or waive a violation of its sovereignty. Furthermore, it makes no difference whether or not the measures by which the accused was brought into the jurisdiction were unlawful in regard to municipal law or international law. The Court will not enter into an examination of this question because it is not relevant to the trial of the accused. The accused has no right to plead a violation of the sovereignty of a state because it is the exclusive right of the state to raise the plea or waive it. In this case, the indictment was filed after Argentina had exonerated Israel (P) of violating Argentina's sovereignty and thus Israel (P) was no longer in any breach of international law. Eichmann (D) therefore cannot presume to speak on behalf of Argentina and claim rights which that sovereign state had waived.

▶ ANALYSIS

This excerpt of the opinion concerns a challenge to jurisdiction based upon the means in which the defendant was brought into the state. The earlier excerpt of the opinion, concerns a challenge to state's jurisdiction based on the crimes not occurring in that state and on the defendant not being a citizen of the state.

■■■

Quicknotes

JURISDICTION The authority of a court to hear and declare judgment in respect to a particular matter.

SOVEREIGNTY The absolute power conferred to the state to govern and regulate all persons located and activities conducted therein.

WAR CRIMES Crimes committed by nations during war in violation of international law.

■■■

United States v. Alvarez-Machain

Federal government (P) v. Foreign national (D)

504 U.S. 655 (1992).

NATURE OF CASE: Review of dismissal of federal indictment.

FACT SUMMARY: Alvarez-Machain (D), abducted from Mexico for trial in the United States (P) by DEA agents, contended that his abduction was illegal because of an extradition treaty between the United States (P) and Mexico.

RULE OF LAW

The presence of an extradition treaty between the United States and another nation does not necessarily preclude obtaining a citizen of that nation through abduction.

FACTS: Alvarez-Machain (Machain) (D) was abducted from his office in Mexico by persons working for DEA agents. He was wanted in the United States (P) for alleged complicity in the torture-murder of a DEA agent. Machain (D) moved to dismiss the indictment, contending that his abduction violated a U.S.-Mexico extradition treaty. The district court agreed and dismissed the indictment. The court of appeals affirmed, and the Supreme Court granted review.

ISSUE: Does the presence of an extradition treaty between the United States and another nation necessarily preclude obtaining a citizen of that nation through abduction?

HOLDING AND DECISION: (Rehnquist, C.J.) No. The presence of an extradition treaty between the United States and another nation does not necessarily preclude obtaining a citizen of that nation through abduction. It has long been the rule that abduction, in and of itself, does not invalidate a prosecution against a foreign national. The only question, therefore, is whether the abduction violates any extradition treaty that may be in effect between the United States (P) and the nation in which the abductee was to be found. Here, the U.S.-Mexican authorities presumably were aware of the United States' (P) longstanding law regarding abductions and did not insist on including a prohibition against abductions. Machain (D) argued that since international law prohibits abductions, so the drafters of the treaty had no reason to consider a prohibition thereof necessary. However, this body of law only applies to situations where no extradition treaty exists, so it is irrelevant here. Consequently, since the extradition treaty does not prohibit abduction such as occurred here, it was not illegal. Reversed.

DISSENT: (Stevens, J.) The treaty at issue provides a detailed treatment of all aspects of extradition between the United States and Mexico. The United States' (P) claim that the treaty is not exclusive, but permits forcible governmental kidnapping, would transform the treaty's provisions into little more than verbiage. Although it is true, as the majority notes, that there is nothing in the treaty that expressly prohibits a contracting party from forcibly abducting suspects in the territory of the other, the manifest scope and object of the treaty itself plainly imply a mutual undertaking to respect the territorial integrity of the other contracting party. The majority's effective conclusion that the treaty's silence on this issue creates an alternative method for obtaining jurisdiction over alleged offenders and permits the parties to resort to self-help would equally permit the United States to engage in torture and execution in lieu of extradition. The majority opinion fails to distinguish between acts of private citizens, which does not violate any treaty obligations, and conduct expressly authorized by the executive branch, which undoubtedly constitutes a fragrant violation of international law and a breach of the U.S. (P) treaty obligations.

ANALYSIS

Machain (D) lost this battle but won the war. He was tried in Los Angeles in 1993. At the close of the prosecution's case, the trial judge, Edward Rafeedie, dismissed the case for lack of evidence. The judge used some harsh language in his order, apparently believing the case should never have been brought.

Quicknotes

EXTRADITION The surrender by one state or nation to another of an individual allegedly guilty of committing a crime in that area.

Prosecutor v. Nikolic, Decision on Interlocutory Appeal Concerning Legality of Arrest

[Parties not identified.]

Case No. IT-94-2-AR73 (2003).

NATURE OF CASE: Violation of state sovereignty in arresting a terrorist by foreign government.

FACT SUMMARY: [Nikolic was abducted by the NATO-led stabilization force in Bosnia, acting in collusion with unknown individuals from Serbia and Montenegro; an issue was whether his kidnapping divested the Appeals Chamber of jurisdiction.]

🏛 RULE OF LAW
When a fugitive accused of a universally condemned offense is apprehended through kidnapping in a foreign state, jurisdiction should not be declined on the ground that there was a violation of the sovereignty of a state or of the accused's human rights.

FACTS: [Nikolic was abducted by the NATO-led stabilization force in Bosnia, acting in collusion with unknown individuals from Serbia and Montenegro; an issue was whether his kidnapping divested the Appeals Chamber of jurisdiction.]

ISSUE: When a fugitive accused of a universally condemned offense is apprehended through kidnapping in a foreign state, should jurisdiction be declined on the ground that there was a violation of the sovereignty of a state or of the accused's human rights?

HOLDING AND DECISION: [Judge not stated in casebook excerpt.] No. When a fugitive accused of a universally condemned offense is apprehended through kidnapping in a foreign state, jurisdiction should not be declined on the ground that there was a violation of the sovereignty of a state or of the accused's human rights. The damage caused to international justice by not apprehending fugitives accused of serious violations of international humanitarian law is higher than the injury, if any, caused to the sovereignty of a state by a limited intrusion into its territory to apprehend the fugitive. In addition, the accused's fundamental human rights must be balanced with the essential interests of the international community in the prosecution of persons charged with serious violations of humanitarian law, and the kidnapping of the accused in this case did not divest the court of jurisdiction.

▶ ANALYSIS

The court does not elaborate on the balancing test it applied to determine that the interests of international justice outweigh the state's interest in sovereignty or the accused's human rights. The focus was mainly on the seriousness of the accused's alleged crimes—though the casebook excerpt does not elaborate on what those crimes were.

■■■

Quicknotes

INTERLOCUTORY APPEAL The appeal of an issue that does not resolve the disposition of the case, but is essential to a determination of the parties' legal rights.

SOVEREIGNTY The absolute power conferred to the state to govern and regulate all persons located and activities conducted therein.

■■■

The Schooner Exchange v. McFaddon

Government (D) v. Claimants (P)

11 U.S. 116 (1812).

NATURE OF CASE: Appeal from reversal of dismissal of claim of ownership.

FACT SUMMARY: Two American citizens (P) claimed they owned and were entitled to possession of the Schooner Exchange.

🏛 RULE OF LAW
National ships of war entering the port of a friendly power are to be considered as exempted by the consent of that power from its jurisdiction.

FACTS: Two American citizens (P) claimed they had seized the Schooner Exchange on the high seas and that they now owned it and were entitled to possession of the ship. The United States Attorney claimed that the United States and France were at peace and that a public ship of the Emperor of France had been compelled by bad weather to enter the port of Philadelphia and was prevented by leaving by process of the court. The district court granted the United States' request to dismiss the claims of ownership and ordered that the ship be released. The circuit court reversed, and the United States (D) appealed to the United States Supreme Court.

ISSUE: Are national ships of war entering the port of a friendly power to be considered as exempted by the consent of that power from its jurisdiction?

HOLDING AND DECISION: (Marshall, C.J.) Yes. National ships of war entering the port of a friendly power are to be considered as exempted by the consent of that power from its jurisdiction. The jurisdiction of the nation within its own territory is exclusive and absolute. The Schooner Exchange, a public armed ship, in the service of a foreign sovereign, with whom the United States is at peace, and having entered a U.S. port open for her reception, must be considered to have come into the American territory, under an implied promise, that while necessarily within it, and demeaning herself in a friendly manner, she should be exempt from the jurisdiction of the country. Reversed.

▶ ANALYSIS

This case implicated the absolute form of sovereign immunity from judicial jurisdiction. The court highlighted three principles: (1) the exemption of the person of the sovereign from arrest or detention within a foreign country; (2) the immunity which all civilized nations allow to foreign ministers; and (3) that a sovereign is understood to cede a portion of his territorial jurisdiction when he allows troops of a foreign prince to pass through his dominions.

Quicknotes

SOVEREIGN IMMUNITY Immunity of government from suit without its consent.

Republic of Argentina v. Weltover, Inc.

Bond issuer (D) v. Bond holders (P)

504 U.S. 607 (1992).

NATURE OF CASE: Review of denial of dismissal of action for breach of contract.

FACT SUMMARY: Argentina (D) contended that it could not be sued in a U.S. court for defaulting on bonds it had issued.

RULE OF LAW
A foreign government may be amenable to suit in a U.S. court for defaulting on its bonds.

FACTS: Due to currency instability, Argentine businesses often had trouble participating in foreign transactions. The Argentine government (D), to ameliorate this problem, instituted a program wherein it agreed to sell to domestic borrowers U.S. dollars in exchange for Argentine currency. The dollars could be used to pay foreign creditors of Argentine businesses. Argentina (D) issued bonds, called "Bonods," to reflect its obligations. In 1986, Argentina (D), facing a shortage of reserves of U.S. dollars, defaulted on bond payments. Several bond holders (P), who collectively owned $1.3 million worth of bonds payable in New York, sued for breach of contract in federal court in New York. Argentina (D) moved to dismiss, asserting sovereign immunity. The district court denied the motion, and the Second Circuit affirmed. The Supreme Court granted review.

ISSUE: May a foreign government be amenable to suit in a U.S. court for defaulting on its bonds?

HOLDING AND DECISION: (Scalia, J.) Yes. A foreign government may be amenable to suit in a U.S. court for defaulting on its bonds. The Foreign Sovereign Immunities Act of 1976 (FSIA) creates an exception to foreign sovereign immunity "commercial" activities. For purposes of the FSIA, an activity falls within the exception if (1) it occurs outside the United States, (2) is in connection with commerce, and (3) causes a direct effect in the United States. Here, the first element without question has been satisfied. Whether a government's activity is "commercial" must be determined with reference to the nature of the act. The issuing of a bond is a commercial rather than a sovereign act—private concerns can and often do issue bonds; it is not an activity given only to sovereigns. Finally, an effect is "direct" if an effect is the natural and immediate consequence of the activity in question. Here, the effect in the United States was direct because the bonds were payable in New York, so the breach occurred there. In sum, the activities of Argentina (D) with respect to the bonds were commercial in nature, so the commercial activity exception to the FSIA applies. Affirmed.

ANALYSIS

The key to determining if the commercial activity exception applies in any given case is whether the government has entered the marketplace. If it has, it is to be treated, under the FSIA, as a private player. If it undertakes an activity peculiar to a sovereign, the exception does not apply.

Quicknotes

BOND A debt instrument issued by the issuing entity evidencing a promise to repay the loan with a specified amount of interest on a particular date.

SOVEREIGN IMMUNITY Immunity of government from suit without its consent.

Saudi Arabia v. Nelson

Host country (D) v. Foreign citizen (P)

507 U.S. 349 (1993).

NATURE OF CASE: Appeal from a judgment for the plaintiff in a personal injury action against a sovereign government.

FACT SUMMARY: Saudi Arabia (D) claimed foreign sovereign immunity from jurisdiction of U.S. federal court in Nelson's (P) suit against the country.

🏛 RULE OF LAW
Foreign states are entitled to immunity from the jurisdiction of courts in the United States, unless the legal action is based on commercial activity.

FACTS: Nelson (P) worked for a hospital in Saudi Arabia (D), and after he repeatedly reported safety defects in the hospital's equipment, the hospital summoned Saudi police, who tortured and imprisoned Nelson (P).

ISSUE: Are foreign states entitled to immunity from the jurisdiction of courts in the United States, unless the legal action is based on commercial activity?

HOLDING AND DECISION: (Souter, J.) Yes. Foreign states are entitled to immunity from the jurisdiction of courts in the United States, unless the legal action is based on commercial activity. Saudi Arabia's (D) conduct fails to qualify as commercial activity, because it was the government police who committed the tortious act. A foreign state's exercise of the police power is sovereign in nature and is not the sort of activity engaged in by private parties.

CONCURRENCE: (White, J.) The hospital has no apparent connection to the United States, and absent that, Nelson (P) does not have access to U.S. courts in this action. However, the fixation by the majority on the intervention of police officers, and the consequential characterization of the conduct as sovereign in nature, is misguided. The hospital summoned Nelson (P) to its security office because he reported safety concerns and the hospital played a part in the beating and imprisonment. That behavior does not qualify as sovereign. At the very least, it consists of both commercial and sovereign elements. Nevertheless, the holding is correct because the commercial activity was not carried on in the United States.

▶ ANALYSIS

Under the "restrictive" as opposed to the "absolute" theory of foreign sovereign immunity, a state is immune from the jurisdiction of foreign courts as to its sovereign or public acts but not as to those that are private or commercial in nature. A state engages in commercial activity under the restrictive theory where it exercises only those powers that can also be exercised by private citizens, as distinct from those powers peculiar to sovereigns. Whether a state acts in the manner of a private party is a question of behavior, not motivation. While it is difficult to distinguish the purpose of conduct from its nature, the Court recognized that the Foreign Sovereign Immunities Act of 1976 unmistakably commands it to observe the distinction.

■■■

Quicknotes

IMMUNITY Exemption from a legal obligation.

SOVEREIGNTY The absolute power conferred to the state to govern and regulate all persons located and activities conducted therein.

■■■

Antares Aircraft, L.P. v. Federal Republic of Nigeria

Private partnership (P) v. Sovereign nation (D)

999 F.2d 33 (2d Cir. 1993).

NATURE OF CASE: Remand of appellate decision affirming sovereign immunity.

FACT SUMMARY: An airplane owned by Antares Aircraft, L.P. (Antares) (P), a U.S. partnership, was detained in Nigeria in order to satisfy airport fees allegedly owed to the Nigerian Airports Authority (NAA) (D). Antares (P) filed suit against the Federal Republic of Nigeria (D) and the NAA (collectively "Federal Republic of Nigeria" (FRN)) (D) in federal district court, claiming that the plane had been detained as part of a scheme to extort payments from Antares (P). FRN (D) moved to dismiss on the basis that it had sovereign immunity.

🏛 RULE OF LAW
A financial loss suffered by a private U.S. entity does not by itself have "a direct effect" in the United States sufficient to trigger the "direct effect" requirement to the commercial activity exception to sovereign immunity.

FACTS: An airplane owned by Antares (P), a U.S. partnership, was detained in Nigeria in order to satisfy airport fees allegedly owed to the Nigerian Airports Authority (NAA) (D), which was wholly owned by the Federal Republic of Nigeria (D). Antares (P) filed suit against FRN and NAA (collectively "FRN") (D) in federal district court, claiming that the plane had been detained as part of a scheme to extort payments from Antares (P). FRN (D) moved to dismiss on the basis that it had sovereign immunity. The district court granted the motion to dismiss, and the court of appeals affirmed. The United States Supreme Court vacated and remanded in light of its decision in *Republic of Argentina v. Weltover, Inc.*, 504 U.S. 607 (1992), for a determination as to whether the detention of the aircraft caused a "direct effect in the United States."

ISSUE: Does a financial loss suffered by a private U.S. entity by itself have "a direct effect" in the United States sufficient to trigger the "direct effect" requirement to the commercial activity exception to sovereign immunity?

HOLDING AND DECISION: (Winter, J.) No. A financial loss suffered by a private U.S. entity does not by itself have "a direct effect" in the United States sufficient to trigger the "direct effect" requirement to the commercial activity exception to sovereign immunity. The final element of the "commercial activity" exception to sovereign immunity requires that the act complained of have a "direct effect" in the United States. Here, the issue is whether the detention of Antares's (P) plane in Nigeria

caused such a direct effect. A foreign tort may have sufficient contacts with the United States to establish the requisite "direct effect." Here, however, all legally significant acts took place in Nigeria, where the detention of the plane (and damage to it) and negotiation and payment of the fees occurred. The fact that the payments originated in New York is not legally significant, because the payments could have come from anywhere; the legally significant fact is that payment had to be made in Nigeria. This is unlike the situation in *Republic of Argentina v. Weltover, Inc.*, 504 U.S. 607 (1992) (which found no sovereign immunity), where a contract was to be performed in the United States, Antares's (P) argument that the requisite "direct effect" was that it suffered a financial loss is rejected. If a loss to a U.S. individual or firm resulting from a foreign tort were sufficient by itself to satisfy the direct effect requirement, the Foreign Sovereign Immunities Act's (FSIA) provision of sovereign immunity would be eviscerated, because most commercial torts can be pled as torts of conversion or fraud, and because any U.S. citizen could bring suit based on personal injury regardless of where it occurred. Reaffirmed.

DISSENT: (Altimari, J.) The appropriate inquiry is whether a private U.S. entity has suffered a "direct" financial loss. The only loss entities such as partnerships and corporations can suffer is financial, and the loss occurs where the entity is formed or its principal place of business is located. An individual, by contrast, suffers a loss where the tort occurs. The majority's reliance on personal injury cases is unpersuasive, especially in light of the Supreme Court's affirmance in *Weltover* and its remand of this case in light of *Weltover*. Accordingly, Antares (P) suffered a "direct effect" in the United States within the meaning of the FSIA.

▶ ANALYSIS

A central purpose of the FSIA was to remove sovereign immunity from certain types of commercial disputes. It seems that the majority in this case gave short shrift to that goal, given that it acknowledged that the detention of the plane and the collection of fees were "in connection with a commercial activity of the foreign state."

▰▭▰

Quicknotes

IMMUNITY Exemption from a legal obligation.

Continued on next page.

SOVEREIGNTY The absolute power conferred to the state to govern and regulate all persons located and activities conducted therein.

TORT A legal wrong resulting in a breach of duty by the wrongdoer, causing damages as a result of the breach.

■━━■

International Human Rights

Quick Reference Rules of Law

Republic of Ireland v. United Kingdom

Government (P) v. Government (D)

Eur. Ct. Human Rights Series A, No. 25 (1978).

NATURE OF CASE: Referral to the court of charges alleging a violation of the European Convention on Human Rights.

FACT SUMMARY: After the United Kingdom (D) subjected fourteen suspects to disorientation and sensory deprivation techniques, Ireland (P) referred the case to the Court of Human Rights, alleging that the techniques constituted torture and inhuman and degrading treatment, violating the European Convention on Human Rights.

> ## 🏛 RULE OF LAW
> Torture and inhuman or degrading treatment are prohibited, irrespective of the victim's conduct.

FACTS: Under the Special Powers Act, the United Kingdom (D) had the right to imprison, without trial, individuals thought to be "suspected terrorists" and "key members of the IRA." The government of Ireland (P) referred the case to the Court of Human Rights, alleging that fourteen suspects had been subjected to techniques constituting torture and inhuman and degrading treatment prohibited by Article 3 of the European Convention on Human Rights, and that internment without trial violated Article 5. Ireland (P) alleged that the United Kingdom (D) used five "disorientation" and "sensory deprivation" techniques. Although the European Commission on Human Rights found that such techniques had been used, the United Kingdom (D) argued that the Court should decline to exercise its jurisdiction since use of the techniques had been abandoned, and steps had been taken to impose punishment for, and prevent the recurrence of, the various violations found by the Commission.

ISSUE: Are torture and inhuman or degrading treatment prohibited, irrespective of the victim's conduct?

HOLDING AND DECISION: [Judge not stated in casebook excerpt.] Yes. Torture and inhuman or degrading treatment are prohibited, irrespective of the victim's conduct. Although the United Kingdom (D) has taken various measures to prevent the recurrence of the events complained of and to afford reparation for their consequences, the court should still rule thereon, since its judgments also serve to elucidate, safeguard, and develop the rules instituted by the Convention. The five techniques were applied in combination, with premeditation and for hours at a stretch. They accordingly fell into the category of inhuman treatment within the meaning of Article 3. The techniques were also degrading, but they did not occasion suffering of the particular intensity and cruelty implied by the word "torture." The sanctions available to the Court, however, do not include the power to direct the United Kingdom (D) to institute criminal or disciplinary proceedings against those who violated Article 3 and those who condoned or tolerated such violations.

▌ANALYSIS

In the Commission's estimation, the techniques employed by the United Kingdom (D) also constituted torture. When a complaint is brought before the Commission, a friendly settlement is attempted through the Commission's conciliation processes. Only if such a settlement attempt fails can the case then be referred to the Court.

■=■

Public Committee Against Torture in Israel v. State of Israel

Human rights group (P) v. Sovereign state (D)

38 I.L.M. 1471 (1999).

NATURE OF CASE: Proceeding before the Israel Supreme Court to determine the legality of interrogation methods.

FACT SUMMARY: Israel's General Security Service (GSS) used what it called "moderate physical pressure" in the interrogation of suspected terrorists. The Public Committee Against Torture in Israel (P), a human rights group, challenged the legality of these methods.

🏛 **RULE OF LAW**
Interrogations of suspected terrorists may not use physical means absent enabling legislation.

FACTS: Israel's General Security Service (GSS) used what it called "moderate physical pressure" in the interrogation of suspected terrorists. The Public Committee Against Torture in Israel (P), a human rights group, challenged the legality of these methods, which included forceful shaking of the suspect's upper torso, prolonged sitting on a low, tilted chair, with hands tied behind the back and head covered by a sack, excessive tightening of handcuffs, and sleep deprivation.

ISSUE: May interrogations of suspected terrorists use physical means absent enabling legislation?

HOLDING AND DECISION: [Judge not stated in casebook excerpt.] Interrogations of suspected terrorists may not use physical means absent enabling legislation. The purpose of GSS interrogations is to gather information to thwart terrorist attacks. Interrogation rules therefore pit two conflicting values against each other. On the one hand is the desire to uncover the truth in order to prevent crime; on the other hand is the desire to protect the suspect's dignity and liberty. The balancing of these values results in a "reasonable interrogation." A reasonable interrogation is free from torture, free of cruel and inhuman treatment, and free of any degrading handling. There is no exception to this rule. However, a reasonable interrogation may be unpleasant and cause discomfort, e.g., sleep deprivation. Shaking is a prohibited investigation method because it harms the suspect's body and violates the suspect's dignity. The law of Israel does not expressly authorize the GSS to employ physical means. Such authority cannot be implied from a necessity defense—on the theory that GSS investigators are authorized to apply physical means in order to prevent serious harm to human life or body that result from terrorists acts—because this defense is applicable to individuals accused of a crime and their ad hoc reaction to an event. Therefore, the defense cannot be used as a source of general administrative power. If Israel wants to enable GSS investigators to use physical means in interrogations, the legislature must pass legislation authorizing such means. Absent such legislation, as a matter of law, such means are not authorized.

▶ **ANALYSIS**

After the Israel Supreme Court rendered its decision, the Israeli government established a commission to consider whether legislation should be passed to permit the GSS to continue to use physical means in interrogations of terrorist suspects. Although such legislation has yet not been promulgated, it seems that if such legislation were to be passed, some physical means, such as shaking, would nevertheless be absolutely proscribed under the Court's decision and international law.

■▬■

Leyla Şahin v. Turkey

Turkish Muslim (P) v. Sovereign state (D)

Eur. Ct. of Human Rights, 2005-XI Eur. Ct. H.R. 173 (2005).

NATURE OF CASE: Application alleging violations of rights and freedoms under the Convention for the Protection of Human Rights and Fundamental Freedoms.

FACT SUMMARY: Şahin (P), a Turkish Muslim, claimed the Republic of Turkey (D) violated her rights and freedoms under the Convention for the Protection of Human Rights and Fundamental Freedoms by banning the wearing of the Islamic headscarf in institutions of higher education.

🏛 RULE OF LAW
The ban by a secular country on wearing religious clothing in institutions of higher education does not violate students' rights and freedoms under the Convention for the Protection of Human Rights and Fundamental Freedoms.

FACTS: Şahin (P) was a medical student at the Istanbul University who wore an Islamic headscarf. Shortly after her enrollment, the Vice-Chancellor of the University issued a circular directing that students with beards and students wearing the Islamic headscarf would be refused admission to lectures, courses and tutorials. Şahin (P) filed an application against the Republic of Turkey (Turkey) (P) with the European Commission of Human Rights (the "Commission") under the Convention for the Protection of Human Rights and Fundamental Freedoms (the "Convention"), alleging that her rights and freedoms under Article 9 of the Convention had been violated by the ban on the wearing of the Islamic headscarf in institutions of higher education. The Grand Chamber of the European Court of Human Rights heard the case and rendered a judgment.

ISSUE: Does the ban by a secular country on wearing religious clothing in institutions of higher education violate students' rights and freedoms under the Convention for the Protection of Human Rights and Fundamental Freedoms?

HOLDING AND DECISION: [Judge not stated in casebook excerpt.] No. The ban by a secular country on wearing religious clothing in institutions of higher education does not violate students' rights and freedoms under the Convention for the Protection of Human Rights and Fundamental Freedoms. Turkey (D) is constitutionally a secular ("laik" in Turkish) state founded on the principles of equality without regard to distinctions based on sex, religion, or denomination. The wearing of the Islamic headscarf in educational institutions is a relatively recent development. The supporters of secularism see the Islamic headscarf as a symbol of a political Islam. The issue presented is whether the ban interfered with Şahin's (P) rights under Article 9, and, if so, whether the interference was "prescribed by law," pursued a legitimate aim and was "necessary in a democratic society." Because Şahin (P) was wearing the headscarf to obey a religious precept, the ban interfered with her right to manifest her religion. This interference was, however, prescribed by Turkish law as interpreted by the Turkish courts. Additionally, the impugned interference primarily pursued the legitimate aims of protecting the rights and freedoms of others and of protecting public order. In democratic societies, in which several religions coexist within the same population, it may be necessary to place restrictions on freedom to manifest one's religion or belief in order to reconcile the interests of the various groups and ensure that everyone's beliefs are respected. The state has a duty to be neutral in ensuring that there is public order, religious harmony and tolerance in a democratic society, and ensuring that there is mutual tolerance between opposing groups. This does not entail the elimination of pluralism, which along with tolerance and broadmindedness, are hallmarks of a democratic society. Instead, this requires a balancing that ensures fair treatment of minorities without abuse of a dominant group, even if individual interests must sometimes be subordinated to those of a group. Where there is great divergence of opinion on certain issues—such as the wearing of an Islamic headscarf—the national decision-making body's role must be given great importance. Rules on such issues may vary greatly from one country to the next according to national traditions and the requirements imposed by the need to protect the rights and freedoms of others and to maintain public order. Each state, therefore, must, to a certain degree, be permitted to decide the extent and form such regulations should take based on the domestic context. This "margin of appreciation" requires the Court to decide whether the measures taken at the national level were justified and proportionate. The Court has previously stressed that the headscarf is a "powerful external symbol" that is hard to reconcile with the principle of gender equality or the message of tolerance, respect for others, and, above all, equality and non-discrimination. Applying these principles here, considering the question of the Islamic headscarf in the Turkish context, it is observed that the wearing of the headscarf may have a great impact on those who choose not to wear it, given that the majority of the population, while professing a strong attachment to the rights of women and a secular way life, are Muslims. The impugned interference therefore serves the

Continued on next page.

key goals of secularism and equality. Additionally, the headscarf has taken on political significance as extremist political movements in Turkey seek to impose on society as a whole their religious symbols and conception of a society founded on religious precepts. Here, the ban serves to preserve pluralism in the university. Accordingly, the objectives of the ban were legitimate. This leads to the issue of whether there was a reasonable relationship of proportionality between the means employed and the legitimate objectives pursued by the interference. In this regard, the Court should not substitute its view for that of the university authorities, who are better placed to evaluate local needs. Article 9 does not always guarantee the right to behave in a manner governed by a religious belief and does not confer on people who do so the right to disregard rules that have proved to be justified. Giving due regard to Turkey's (P) margin of appreciation, the interference here was justified in principle and proportionate to the aim pursued. Therefore, Article 9 has not been breached.

▶ *ANALYSIS*

"Margin of appreciation" is the word-for-word English translation of the French phrase "marge d'appreciation," a concept used in a number of courts in Europe, among them the Strasbourg human rights court and the European Union courts in Luxembourg. It means, roughly, the range of discretion. As this case demonstrates, it is a concept the European Court of Human Rights has developed when considering whether a signatory of the European Convention on Human Rights has breached the declaration. The margin of appreciation doctrine allows the court to account for the fact that the Convention will be interpreted differently in different signatory states, so that judges are obliged to take into account the cultural, historic and philosophical contexts of the particular nation in question.

■=■

Dissenting Opinion of Judge Tulkens
[in the case of Leyla Şahin v. Turkey]

[Turkish Muslim (P) v. Sovereign state (D)]

Eur. Ct. of Human Rights, 2005-XI Eur. Ct. H.R. 220 (2005).

[NOTE: See the brief on page 60 (Leyla Şahin v. Turkey, Eur. Ct. of Human Rights, 2005-XI Eur. Ct. H.R. 173 [2005]), for the facts, rule, issue, and holding and decision by the majority of the Court's Grand Chamber in this case.]

DISSENT: (Tulkens, J.) Freedom to manifest a religion means that everyone is allowed to exercise that right, whether individually or collectively, in public or in private, subject to the dual condition that they do not infringe the rights and freedoms of others and do not prejudice public order. There was no evidence here that Şahin's (P) wearing of the headscarf was intended to violate or caused the violation of either of these conditions. There was no evidence that the headscarf worn by Şahin (P) was intended to proselytize, spread propaganda, or undermine others' convictions, or that there was any disruption in teaching or in everyday life at the University, or any disorderly conduct, that resulted from her wearing the headscarf. The possible effect on others who do not wear it or believe in it does not implicate a pressing social need. Moreover, the Court has never accepted that interference with the exercise of the right to freedom of expression can be justified by the fact that the ideas or views concerned are not shared by everyone and may even offend some people. In fact, the Court finds justification for the ban on the need to mitigate the threat posed by "extremists." While everyone agrees on the need to prevent radical Islamism, there has not been a showing that wearing a headscarf is associated with fundamentalism. Not all women who wear the headscarf are extremists. Additionally, the majority's assertion that the ban on the headscarf promotes sexual equality is not supported. Wearing the headscarf does not necessarily symbolize the submission of women to men, and some even argue that it is an indication of women's emancipation. What is missing from the argument is the opinion of women, both those who wear the headscarf and those who do not. It is not for the Court to appraise a religion or a religious practice, and, specifically, it should not impose its viewpoint on Şahin (P). The Court does not articulate how the principle of sexual equality can justify prohibiting a woman from following a practice which, in the absence of proof to the contrary, she must be presumed to have freely adopted. Equality and non-discrimination are subjective rights which must remain under the control of those who are entitled to benefit from them, and which is codified in Article 8 as the right of personal autonomy. In any event, if wearing the headscarf was truly contrary to the principle of equality between men and women, the State would have a positive obligation to prohibit it in all places, whether public or private.

▶ *ANALYSIS*

As Judge Tulkens suggests, some have argued that legal restrictions on veiling can free women from coercive social and community pressures to wear the veil. Others, on the other hand argue that it is a mistake to assume that all those who wear the veil are forced to do so, and that the consequences of restrictive legislation could be drastic, since those who are unwilling or unable to walk in public without a full veil could be confined to their homes. These arguments demonstrate the difficulty of crafting rules that both promote equality and social cohesion while respecting cultural and religious differences, and the debate over the headscarf thus continues in Turkey and other states.

R (Begum) v. Headteacher and Governors of Denbigh High School

Muslim student (P) v. School administrators (D)

United Kingdom House of Lords, [2006] UKHL 15 (2006).

NATURE OF CASE: Case under the European Convention on Human Rights for interference with the manifestation of one's religion.

FACT SUMMARY: Begum (P), a Muslim teenager, contended that her rights under the European Convention on Human Rights were violated when her high school's authorities refused to let her wear the jilbab and insisted that she adhere to the school's dress code, which included some Muslim attire.

RULE OF LAW

Interference with a manifestation of one's religion is justified where it has the aim of protecting the rights and freedoms of others and is proportionate to that aim.

FACTS: Begum (P), a Muslim teenager, sought permission from her high school's authorities (D) to wear the jilbab, a long gown that conceals the shape of the arms and legs. The school, which was predominantly Muslim but welcomed students of other faiths, had adopted a dress code policy providing students with three choices of school uniform. One was the shalwar kameeze, a traditional form of attire in South Asia. The school chose its uniforms after consulting local mosques, parents, and community organizations. Begum stated that the shalwar kameeze chosen by the school was too close fitting and that the jilbab would better suit the modesty requirements of her faith. The school authorities (D) denied her request, stating that the uniforms were chosen to promote social cohesion while respecting cultural and religious differences. The authorities (D) also expressed concern that allowing the jilbab would put pressure on other girls to wear it against their wishes. Begum (P) brought a case under the European Convention on Human Rights, asserting that her religious rights had been violated. The House of Lords heard and decided the case.

ISSUE: Is interference with a manifestation of one's religion justified where it has the aim of protecting the rights and freedoms of others and is proportionate to that aim?

HOLDING AND DECISION: (Hale, Lady) Yes. Interference with a manifestation of one's religion is justified where it has the aim of protecting the rights and freedoms of others and is proportionate to that aim. The restrictions here must be distinguished from those that might be imposed on Muslim women. In the school context, where the school's task is to educate the young from all the many and diverse families and communities in accordance with the national curriculum and to help each student reach his or her potential, the school must be able to promote harmony among students of diverse races, religions, and cultures. A uniform dress code can help smooth over ethnic, religious and social divisions, and, in a society committed to equal freedom for men and women to choose how they will lead their lives within the law, such a code can help young girls from ethnic, cultural or religious minorities determine how far to adopt or distance themselves from the dominant culture. Here, the school authorities (D) have struck the right balance between giving girls a chance to decide whether they will adopt the more feminist dominant culture, and respecting individual autonomy and cultural diversity of parents as well as students.

ANALYSIS

In Britain, which protect a woman's right to choose whether to wear a headscarf in the non-school setting, it has been held that the rejection of an applicant for a job in a hairdressing salon because she wore a headscarf constituted impermissible employment discrimination. However, it has also been held that it is legitimate to bar a school support worker from wearing a veil while teaching, to promote the effective education of her students. These decisions seem to turn on some of the considerations articulated by Lady Hale in her opinion.

International Humanitarian Law

Quick Reference Rules of Law

Legality of the Threat or Use of Nuclear Weapons

[Parties not identified.]

1996 I.C.J. 226 (July 8).

NATURE OF CASE: Advisory opinion examining whether the threat or use of nuclear weapons is permitted under international law.

FACT SUMMARY: The United Nations General Assembly solicited an advisory opinion from the International Court of Justice (ICJ) regarding the legality of the threat or use of nuclear weapons.

🏛 RULE OF LAW
Although international humanitarian law regarding armed conflict and the law of neutrality is applicable to the question of whether recourse to nuclear weapons is illegal and such a threat or use of nuclear weapons would generally be contrary to the rules of international law, the present state of the law does not give a definitive conclusion as to the legality or illegality of the threat or use of nuclear weapons by a state in self-defense, in which the very survival of the state would be at stake.

FACTS: Non-Governmental Organizations (NGOs) committed to the elimination of nuclear weapons formed the World Court Project in an effort to elicit an opinion from the ICJ declaring that the use of nuclear weapons would be illegal in all circumstances. The United Nations General Assembly subsequently solicited an advisory opinion from the Court.

ISSUE: Is the threat or use of nuclear weapons in any circumstance permitted under international law?

HOLDING AND DECISION: [Judge not stated in casebook excerpt.] Although international humanitarian law regarding armed conflict and the law of neutrality is applicable to the question of whether recourse to nuclear weapons is illegal and such a threat or use of nuclear weapons would generally be contrary to the rules of international law, the present state of the law does not give a definitive conclusion as to the legality or illegality of the threat or use of nuclear weapons by a state in self-defense, in which the very survival of the state would be at stake The applicable law to decide the issue is the law relating to the use of force as enshrined in the United Nations Charter and the law applicable in armed conflict which regulates the conduct of hostilities, together with any specific treaties on nuclear weapons that are relevant. The Charter neither expressly prohibits, nor permits, the use of any specific weapon. The principles and rules of international humanitarian law are aimed at the protection of the civilian population and civilian objects and establishes the distinction between combatants and non-combatants. According to the law, states must never make civilians the object of

attack and must consequently never use weapons that are incapable of distinguishing between civilian and military targets. In addition, there is a prohibition against causing unnecessary suffering to combatants and against using weapons that will cause them such harm or aggravate their suffering. States, therefore, do not have unlimited freedom of choice of means in the weapons they use. The fact that recourse to nuclear weapons is subject to and regulated by the law of armed conflict does not necessarily mean, however, that such recourse is prohibited. Furthermore, a number of specific treaties have been enacted to limit the acquisition, manufacture, possession, deployment, and testing of nuclear weapons. The existence of these treaties does not mean, however, that the recourse to nuclear weapons is illegal. The treaties point to an increasing concern in the international community with these weapons and foreshadow a future general prohibition of the use of such weapons, but they do not constitute such a prohibition by themselves. Neither do other treaties, which state intent not to use nuclear weapons in certain zones but to reserve the right to use them in certain circumstances, amount to a comprehensive and universal conventional prohibition on the use, or the threat of use, of nuclear weapons. Moreover, nuclear weapons are not prohibited under Hague and Geneva Conventions provisions outlawing poisonous weapons because a nuclear weapon's effect is not to poison or asphyxiate. In addition, the law against genocide as continued in the Convention of December 9, 1948, on the Prevention and Punishment of the Crime of Genocide would only apply depending on the circumstances of each case as to whether the recourse of nuclear weapons did entail the intent toward a group. Therefore, a conventional rule of general scope does not exist, nor does a customary rule specifically proscribing the threat or use of nuclear weapons.

DISSENT: (Schwebel, J.) The states that represent the bulk of the world's military, economic, and technological power view the threat of or use of nuclear weapons as lawful in some instances. The Nuclear Non-Proliferation Treaty and other treaties governing acquisition, manufacture, possession, deployment, and testing of nuclear weapons acknowledge that the threat or use of such weapons would not be per se unlawful. With regard to international humanitarian law, it does govern the use of nuclear weapons and concludes that in some circumstances certain uses of nuclear weapons might be lawful and in others not. For instance, their use would be lawful when proportionality in the application of force is correct and discrimination between military and civilian targets is made. Moreover, contemporary events, such as what

Continued on next page.

occurred on the eve of Desert Storm, demonstrate the legality and desirability of the threat of the use of nuclear weapons. Iraq had demonstrated that it was prepared to use weapons of mass destruction. The United States Secretary of State promised Iraq's Foreign Minister that if Iraq used weapons of mass destruction against American forces, the American people would demand vengeance and the United States would use its means to extract it by eliminating the Iraq regime. The President of the United States decided that the best deterrent to the use of weapons of mass destruction by Iraq was the United States' own threat to go after its regime with nuclear weapons, although the President didn't intend to really do so. Subsequently, there was no confirmed use by Iraq of chemical weapons during the war. The Secretary of State's actions cannot be considered as unlawful as the principles of the United Nations Charter were sustained rather than transgressed by the threat.

DISSENT: (Weeramantry, J.) The threat or use of nuclear weapons would not be lawful in any circumstance whatsoever because it offends the fundamental principles of unnecessary suffering both immediate and lingering, proportionality error, discrimination between armed forces and civilians, non-belligerent/innocent states, genocide, environmental damage and human rights. This is true no less in self-defense than in an open act of aggression and also applies to limited, tactical or battlefield nuclear weapons.

DISSENT: (Higgins, J.) The majority has reached a conclusion incompatible with humanitarian law and then refused to decide the issue based on the claim of an absence of a clear legal rule (non liquet) as to whether the use of nuclear weapons in self-defense when the survival of a state is at issue, might still be lawful even where the particular use to be contrary to humanitarian law. This analysis by the majority leaves open the possibility that some use contrary to humanitarian law might be acceptable and such a conclusion goes beyond anything claimed by the states possessing nuclear weapons before the Court. Moreover, the current state of international law is not a justifiable reason for the majority's conclusion because they suggest that a false tension exists between the widespread acceptance of nuclear weapons by states and humanitarian law. If the states believe that the use of such weapons under certain circumstances is acceptable under the Charter, then they believe that they are not violating humanitarian law. Furthermore, although there may be a clash between various elements in the law, it is the role of the judge to decide which norm is preferred in a particular case.

▶ *ANALYSIS*

It is the view of the vast majority of states as well as writers that there can be no doubt as to the applicability of humanitarian law to nuclear weapons. As the opinion states, however, it will be the fruits of the good faith negations, as required by Article VI of the Treaty on the Non-Proliferation of Nuclear Weapons, which will lead to a nuclear disarmament and settle the question at issue in this case.

Quicknotes

GENEVA CONVENTION International agreement that governs the conduct of warring nations.

HAGUE SERVICE CONVENTION Multilateral treaty governing service of process in foreign jurisdictions.

Prosecutor v. Tadic, Jurisdiction Appeal

International prosecutor (P) v. Alleged war criminal (D)

International Criminal Tribunal for the Former Yugoslavia, Appeals Chamber, Case No. IT-94-1-AR72 (1995).

NATURE OF CASE: Appeal from trial chamber decision granting jurisdiction to the International Criminal Tribunal for the Former Yugoslavia over an accused war criminal.

FACT SUMMARY: [Tadic (D), a Bosnian Serb who allegedly took part in ethnic cleansing attacks against civilians during the struggle for control of Bosnia, was indicted by the International Criminal Tribunal for the Former Yugoslavia (ICTY) (P) for numerous violations of international humanitarian law. Tadic (D) contended that the ICTY (P) did not have jurisdiction over him because the Bosnian conflict was internal, rather than international, and, therefore, he could not be charged with grave breaches of the Geneva Conventions for his acts during such an internal struggle.]

🏛 RULE OF LAW
An alleged war criminal may be charged with violations of the laws and customs of war for atrocities committed during an internal armed conflict.

FACTS: [Tadic (D), a Bosnian Serb, allegedly took part in ethnic cleansing attacks against civilians during the struggle for control of Bosnia. Tadic (D) was subsequently arrested in Germany, where he was living, and was accused of committing torture and aiding in the commission of genocide, both crimes under German law. The International Criminal Tribunal for the Former Yugoslavia (ICTY) (P) indicted Tadic (D), alleging numerous violations of international humanitarian law, and requested that Germany defer to the ICTY's (P) jurisdiction over Tadic (D). Germany agreed, and transferred Tadic (D) to the Tribunal (P). Tadic (D) argued that the Tribunal (P) did not have jurisdiction over him because the Bosnian conflict was internal rather than international. From this he argued that any violations of human dignity during the "internal" conflict could not constitute either grave breaches of the Geneva Conventions under Article 2 of the Tribunal's (P) statute or violations of the laws and customs of war entailing individual criminal responsibility under Article 3. The Appeals Chamber found that some of the conflict was international in nature whereas some of it was internal, and agreed with Tadic (D) that as to those parts of the conflict that were internal at the time and place of his acts, he could not be charged with grave breaches of the Geneva Conventions. The Appeals Chamber also addressed whether he could be charged with violations of the laws and customs of war for atrocities in an internal conflict.]

ISSUE: May an alleged war criminal be charged with violations of the laws and customs of war for atrocities committed during an internal armed conflict?

HOLDING AND DECISION: [Judge not stated in casebook excerpt.] Yes. An alleged war criminal may be charged with violations of the laws and customs of war for atrocities committed during an internal armed conflict. Traditional international law did not regulate internal conflicts. However, since the 1930s, the trend has been for increased international regulation of internal armed conflicts. This has resulted in a state-sovereignty-oriented approach being gradually supplanted by a human-being-oriented approach, and the distinction between interstate conflicts and internal conflicts is greatly diminished. This development has brought about the emergence of both customary laws and treaty laws that govern internal strife. In fact, as with Article 3 of the Geneva Conventions, treaty law has become customary law. In this fashion, many principles applicable to international armed conflicts have been extended to internal conflicts, covering both the protection of civilians and the means and methods of warfare. Thus, out of considerations of fundamental human rights, acts that would be prohibited in conflicts between states are also prohibited in internal conflicts. Accordingly, it is established that customary rules have developed to govern internal strife. These rules cover such areas as protection of civilians from hostilities, in particular from indiscriminate attacks, protection of civilian objects, in particular cultural property, protection of all those who do not (or no longer) take active part in hostilities, as well as prohibition of means of warfare proscribed in international armed conflicts and ban of certain methods of conducting hostilities. [Although the trial chamber eventually acquitted Tadic (D) of the charges brought against him under Article 2 for grave breaches, it convicted him of numerous charges brought under Article 3.]

▶ ANALYSIS

The Appeals Chamber listed several reasons for the increased blurring of the distinction between interstate conflicts and internal conflicts for purposes of international law. One is that civil wars have become more frequent, not only because technological progress has made it easier for groups of individuals to have access to weaponry but also on account of increasing tension, whether ideological, interethnic or economic. Another is that internal armed conflicts have become more and more cruel and protracted, involving the whole population of the state where they occur: the all-out resort to armed violence has taken on such a magnitude that the difference with international wars has increasingly dwindled. Yet another is that the large-scale nature of civil strife, coupled with the increasing interdependence of states in the world community, has made it more and more difficult

Continued on next page.

for third-party states to remain aloof: the economic, political and ideological interests of third-party states have brought about direct or indirect involvement of these states in internal conflicts. Finally, the impetuous development and propagation in the international community of human rights doctrines, particularly after the adoption of the Universal Declaration of Human Rights in 1948, has brought about significant changes in international law.

■■■■

Quicknotes

GENEVA CONVENTION   International agreement that governs the conduct of warring nations.

GENOCIDE   The systematic killing of a particular group.

■■■■

Prosecutor v. Tadic, Judgment

International prosecutor (P) v. Alleged war criminal (D)

International Criminal Tribunal for the Former Yugoslavia, Appeals Chamber, Case No. IT-94-1-A (1999).

NATURE OF CASE: Appeal from trial chamber decision dismissing all counts brought under Article 2 of the International Criminal Tribunal for the Former Yugoslavia statute for grave breaches of the Geneva Conventions.

FACT SUMMARY: [Tadic (D), a Bosnian Serb who allegedly took part in ethnic cleansing attacks against civilians during the struggle for control of Bosnia, was indicted by the International Criminal Tribunal for the Former Yugoslavia (ICTY) (P) for numerous violations of international humanitarian law. The trial chamber dismissed all counts under Article 2 of the Tribunal's (P) statute for grave breaches of the Geneva Convention. The prosecution appealed.]

RULE OF LAW

The degree of authority or control that must be wielded by a foreign state over armed forces fighting on its behalf in order to render international an armed conflict that is prima facie internal is such that the state has a role in organizing, coordinating or planning the military actions of the military group, in addition to financing, training and equipping or providing operational support to that group.

FACTS: [Tadic (D), a Bosnian Serb, allegedly took part in ethnic cleansing attacks against civilians during the struggle for control of Bosnia. The International Criminal Tribunal for the Former Yugoslavia (ICTY) (P) indicted Tadic (D), alleging numerous violations of international humanitarian law, including counts brought under Article 2 of the Tribunal's (P) statute for grave breaches of the Geneva Conventions. The trial chamber dismissed all these counts. The Appeals Chamber granted review.]

ISSUE: Is the degree of authority or control that must be wielded by a foreign state over armed forces fighting on its behalf in order to render international an armed conflict that is prima facie internal such that the state has a role in organizing, coordinating or planning the military actions of the military group, in addition to financing, training and equipping or providing operational support to that group?

HOLDING AND DECISION: [Judge not stated in casebook excerpt.] Yes. The degree of authority or control that must be wielded by a foreign state over armed forces fighting on its behalf in order to render international an armed conflict that is prima facie internal is such that the state has a role in organizing, coordinating or planning the military actions of the military group, in addition to financing, training and equipping or providing operational support to that group. It is undisputed that for Article 2 to apply, the conflict must be international in nature. An armed conflict is international if it is between two states. It may also turn into an international conflict where another state intervenes in that conflict through its troops, or, alternatively, if some of the participants in the internal armed conflict act on behalf of that other state. Here it is asserted that the conflict was always between two states—Bosnia and Herzegovina vs. the Federal Republic of Yugoslavia (FRY). This raises the issue of when armed forces fighting against the central authorities of the same state in which they live and operate may be deemed to act on behalf of another state. The criteria for lawful combatants found in the Third Geneva Convention of 1949 provide a useful starting point. These criteria provide that militias or paramilitary groups may be regarded as lawful combatants if they form "part of [the] armed forces of a Party to the conflict. To "belong" to a Party requires that the Party exercise control over the combatants, as well as a relationship of dependence and allegiance by the combatants to the Party. The question then becomes what degree of control by the state is necessary. The answer is not available in international humanitarian law. Therefore, general international law must be looked to. The International Court of Justice (ICJ) previously held that a high degree of control, or effective control, is necessary in the case of individuals or unorganized groups of individuals acting on behalf of the state. However, this standard is insufficiently flexible to render states accountable for the actions of certain combatants, such as military or paramilitary groups, over which the state does not exercise such a degree of control. Where armed forces or militias or paramilitary units are involved, the control required by international law may be deemed to exist when a state or party to the conflict has a role in organizing, coordinating or planning the military actions of the military group, in addition to providing financing, equipment, and operational support. [The Appeals Chamber decided that the FRY had continued to exercise the requisite control over its military units, and, hence, the court held that the conflict was international in character and that the "grave breaches" regime under Article 2 was applicable. Accordingly, it reversed the trial chamber as to this issue.]

ANALYSIS

Under the Appeals Chamber's control test, if the controlling state is not the territorial state where the armed clashes occur or where at any rate the armed units perform their acts, more extensive and compelling evidence is required to show that the state is genuinely in control of the units or groups not merely by financing and equipping them, but also by generally directing or helping plan their actions. The same substantial evidence is required when, although the

Continued on next page.

state in question is the territorial state where armed clashes occur, the general situation is one of turmoil, civil strife and weakened state authority. Where the controlling state in question is an adjacent state with territorial ambitions on the state where the conflict is taking place, and the controlling state is attempting to achieve its territorial enlargement through the armed forces which it controls, it may be easier to establish the threshold.

■━■

Legal Consequences of the Construction of a Wall in the Occupied Palestinian Territory

United Nations (P) v. Israel (D)

2004 I.C.J. 131 (July 9).

NATURE OF CASE: Advisory opinion by International Court Justice (ICJ).

FACT SUMMARY: Israel (D) constructed a wall in occupied Palestinian territory and the United Nations (P) objected.

🏛 RULE OF LAW
The construction of a wall by Israel, the occupying power, in the occupied Palestinian territory, violates international law, including the Fourth Geneva Convention of 1949, the Hague Convention, and relevant Security Council and General Assembly resolutions.

FACTS: Israel (D) constructed a wall in occupied Palestinian territory. The wall and its route impaired the freedom of the Palestinian population. The United Nations General Assembly (P) demanded that it stop and reverse the construction of the wall. The ICJ was asked to provide an advisory opinion on the matter.

ISSUE: Does the construction of a wall by Israel (D), the occupying power, in the occupied Palestinian territory, violate international law, including the Fourth Geneva Convention of 1949, the Hague Convention, and relevant Security Council and General Assembly resolutions?

HOLDING AND DECISION: [Judge not stated in casebook excerpt.] Yes. The construction of a wall by Israel (D), the occupying power, in the occupied Palestinian territory, violates international law, including the Fourth Geneva Convention of 1949, the Hague Convention, and relevant Security Council and General Assembly resolutions. The wall and the Israeli (D) occupation impede the liberty of movement of the inhabitants of the occupied territory, with the exception of Israeli citizens, as guaranteed under Article 12 of the International Covenant on Civil and Political Rights. It also impedes access to work, health facilities, education, and an adequate standard of living under the International Covenant on Economic, Social and Cultural Rights and the United Nations Convention on the Rights of the Child. Finally, the wall changed the demography of the territory, because of the departure of some Palestinians, which violates Article 49 of the Fourth Geneva Convention. Construction of the wall also breaches Israel's (D) obligations under the Fourth Geneva Convention and the Hague Convention because the route chosen for the wall infringes the rights of Palestinians in the occupied territory, which cannot be justified by military exigencies or the requirement of national security. The legal consequence of Israel's (D) actions in the matter is that all states are under an obligation not to recognize the illegal situation resulting from the construction of the wall, and all the states parties to the Fourth Geneva Convention are under an obligation to ensure compliance by Israel (D) with international humanitarian law. Finally, both Israel (D) and Palestine are under an obligation to observe the rules of international humanitarian law. Illegal action and unilateral decisions have been taken on all sides, and implementation of the relevant Security Council resolutions is the only way to end the hostile situation.

SEPARATE OPINION: (Higgins, J.) The ICJ looked at only a part of a much larger conflict between the two states, and should have considered the bigger picture and spelled out what is required of both parties. Of paramount importance is the protection of civilians. In addition, the real impediment to Palestine's ability to exercise its rights as a self-determined peopled is not the wall, but Israel's (D) refusal to withdraw from Arab occupied territory and for Palestine to provide conditions to allow Israel (D) to feel secure in doing so. Further while the wall seems to have resulted in a lessening of attacks on Israeli civilians, the necessity and proportionality for the route selected, balanced against the hardships for Palestinians, have not been explained.

DISSENT: (Buergenthal, J.): The construction of the wall raises important issues of humanitarian law, but the Court should have declined to issue an advisory opinion because the Court failed to address Israel's (D) arguments that it was willing to provide compensation and services for Palestinian residents, and that the wall was intended to be a temporary structure. The Court's conclusions are not convincing, because it failed to demonstrate adequately why it was not convinced that military exigencies and concern for security required Israel (D) to erect the wall along the chosen route.

▶ ANALYSIS

Judge Buergenthal, the only dissenter in the matter, is a U.S. citizen. In addition, the United States was one of eight votes against asking the ICJ for an advisory opinion. Ninety members voted in favor of the opinion, and 74 members abstained.

━━■

Quicknotes

GENEVA CONVENTION International agreement that governs the conduct of warring nations.

HAGUE SERVICE CONVENTION Multilateral treaty governing service of process in foreign jurisdictions.

━━■

Beit Sourik Village Council v. Israel

Indigenous population of the occupied territory (P) v. Occupying state (D)

HCJ 2056/04 (2004).

NATURE OF CASE: Action in Israeli court over Israeli erection of security wall.

FACT SUMMARY: The Israeli Defense Force (D) tried to seize plots of land in the West Bank in order to build a fence to keep terrorists out.

🏛 RULE OF LAW

The authority of the military commander of a state engaged in belligerent occupation must be proportionately balanced against the rights, needs, and interests of the local population.

FACTS: Israel (D) determined that the security of its nation required the erection of a fence around its territory, including that occupied by the country. The fence would separate many indigenous farmers from the local population from their land–specifically, more than 13,000 farmers would be separated by the fence from much of their land and tens of thousands of trees, which are their livelihood.

ISSUE: Must the authority of the military commander of a state engaged in belligerent occupation be proportionately balanced against the rights, needs, and interests of the local population?

HOLDING AND DECISION: [Barak, J.] Yes. The authority of the military commander of a state engaged in belligerent occupation must be proportionately balanced against the rights, needs, and interests of the local population. Israel (D) seeks to build the fence for a legal purpose—security for the people and property of the State—and not for political purposes, which would be illegal under international law. But even if the fence is pursued for security, its benefits must be weighed against the costs. While the security needs are likely to necessitate an injury to the lands of the local inhabitants and to their ability to use them, international humanitarian law requires making every possible effort to ensure that the injury will be proportionate. Here, the impact of the fence on the local population would be severe, and would violate the farmers' rights under humanitarian international law. The injuries are not proportionate and can be substantially decreased by an alternate route for the fence.

▶ ANALYSIS

This opinion by the Israeli Supreme Court was issued a week before the International Court of Justice (ICJ) ruled that military exigencies did not justify Israel's (D) destruction of property to build the fence, or its choice of a route. By reaching the same conclusion as the ICJ in advance of the ICJ's opinion, Israel (D) preserves its sovereignty and prevents political unrest among its own people and in the international community.

Quicknotes

SOVEREIGNTY The absolute power conferred to the state to govern and regulate all persons located and activities conducted therein.

International Criminal Law and Beyond

Quick Reference Rules of Law

United States v. Joseph Alstoetter et al.

Allied country (P) v. War criminals (D)

3 Trials of War Criminals before the Nuernberg Tribunals under Control Council Law No. 10, at 954 (1948).

NATURE OF CASE: Trial before the Nuernberg Tribunals of Nazi judges and prosecutors (D).

FACT SUMMARY: Nazi judges and prosecutors (D) were accused of using the court system against political prisoners, Jews, and other targets, and were prosecuted for war crimes and crimes against humanity. The defendants claimed protection under the principle *nullum crimen sine lege.*

RULE OF LAW
The principle *nullum crimen sine lege* cannot be used to bar prosecution of acts that were crimes under international and domestic law when committed.

FACTS: After World War II, the Allies organized trials in their zones of occupation in Germany. One of these trials, the so-called *Justice Case,* was tried in the American zone under the terms of Law No. 10 promulgated by the Control Council that was officially governing occupied Germany. The 14 defendants were leading Nazi judges and prosecutors (D) who were accused of using the court system against political prisoners, Jews, and other targets, often leading to death sentences. They were prosecuted for war crimes and crimes against humanity. The defendants claimed protection under the principle *nullum crimen sine lege.*

ISSUE: Can the principle *nullum crimen sine lege* be used to bar prosecution of acts that were crimes under international and domestic law when committed?

HOLDING AND DECISION: [Judge not stated in casebook excerpt.] No. The principle *nullum crimen sine lege* cannot be used to bar prosecution of acts that were crimes under international and domestic law when committed. First, the *ex post facto* rule, which condemns statutes that define as criminal those acts committed before the law is passed, is limited in application to statutory law and is inapplicable in international law, because international law is not the product of statute. The principle *nullum crimen sine lege* is a general principle of justice and can be applied to those who violate international treaties because when the actor violates a treaty, he must know that he is violating it. The Nazis knew that their mass murders of Jews was wrong and in contravention of the criminal laws of every civilized state. Moreover, many of the human rights laws of the Weimar era that preceded the Nazi regime were never repealed, so that many of the acts constituting war crimes or crimes against humanity were committed or permitted in direct violation of German law. Thus, the principle *nullum crimen sine lege* cannot be used as a defense when the actor knew that his act was a punishable crime under his own domestic law. Also, under international law, this principle requires that the accused knew or should have known that he was participating in wrongdoing that shocks the conscience of mankind and that he would be punished for his acts. Here, notice of intent to punish was made known by the Allies and the principle of personal responsibility was recognized in international law many years before World War II in the Versailles Treaty.

ANALYSIS

The legitimacy of the Allied tribunals was challenged on the ground that only the losers were tried, and that Allied atrocities were not likewise brought to justice.

Case Concerning the Application of the Convention on the Prevention and Punishment of the Crime of Genocide (Bosnia and Herzegovina v. Serbia and Montenegro)

Civil-war state (P) v. Civil-war state (D)

Int'l Ct. of Justice, 2007 I.C.J. 18 (Feb. 26).

NATURE OF CASE: Action under the Genocide Convention for genocide, conspiracy to commit genocide, complicity in genocide, and failure to prevent genocide

FACT SUMMARY: [Bosnia-Herzegovina (P) contended that Serbia (D) was liable under the Genocide Convention for genocide, conspiracy to commit genocide, complicity in genocide, and failure to prevent genocide in Bosnia based on atrocities that occurred during Bosnia's civil war.]

> 🏛 **RULE OF LAW**
> For there to be genocide, there must be a specific intent to destroy, in whole or in part, an ethnic, religious, or racial group.

FACTS: [Bosnia-Herzegovina (P) contended that Serbia (D) was liable under the Genocide Convention for genocide, conspiracy to commit genocide, complicity in genocide, and failure to prevent genocide in Bosnia based on atrocities that occurred during Bosnia's civil war, including the massacre of some 5,000 to 8,000 Bosnian men and boys at Srebrenica in July 1995. The International Court of Justice (ICJ) set forth its opinion on the intent element of genocide.]

ISSUE: For there to be genocide, must there be a specific intent to destroy, in whole or in part, an ethnic, religious, or racial group?

HOLDING AND DECISION: [Judge not stated in casebook excerpt.] Yes. For there to be genocide, there must be a specific intent to destroy, in whole or in part, an ethnic, religious, or racial group. It is not enough to prove that there have been deliberate unlawful killings of members of such a group. The specific intent, or *dolus specialis*, to destroy the group must accompany such killings. Discriminatory intent is also insufficient. Genocide is an extreme form of persecution, which is based on discriminatory intent. Also, ethnic cleansing—the rendering of an area ethnically homogeneous by using force or intimidation to remove persons of a given group or groups from that area— is not necessarily genocide, since with ethnic cleansing there is not necessarily the intent to destroy the group. Instead, the intent can be to deport or to displace. However, if such displacement is intended to be accompanied by conditions of life calculated to bring about the physical destruction of the group, then ethnic cleansing will rise to the level of genocide. [The ICJ held that the massacre of the Bosnian men and boys was an act of genocide because it was committed with intent to destroy a protected group in whole or in part. However, it also held that Serbia (D) was only responsible for failure to prevent genocide, but was not responsible for the other claims.]

▶ ANALYSIS

The Genocide Convention expressly covers national, ethnic, racial or religious groups. However, it has been argued that the Convention's intent was broader, and should cover political, social, and any other stable and permanent groups. Regardless of which groups are included, this case makes clear that there must be intent to destroy the group, in whole or in part, for the perpetrating party to be responsible for genocide.

Quicknotes

GENOCIDE The systematic killing of a particular group.

Prosecutor v. Erdemovic, Sentencing Appeal

Prosecutor (P) v. Convicted war criminal (D)

Case No. IT-96-22 (1997).

NATURE OF CASE: Appeal of sentence before the International Criminal Tribunal for the Former Yugoslavia (ICTY) for crimes against humanity.

FACT SUMMARY: [Drazen Erdemovic (D) was sentenced to ten years in prison for crimes against humanity. He appealed on the ground of duress.]

🏛 RULE OF LAW
Duress is not a complete defense in international law to the killing of innocents.

FACTS: [Drazen Erdemovic (D) was sentenced to ten years in prison for crimes against humanity for his role as a Bosnian Serb in the massacre of thousands of innocents. He appealed on the ground of duress, claiming that he would have been killed along with his victims had he not killed them.]

ISSUE: Is duress a complete defense in international law to the killing of innocents?

HOLDING AND DECISION: [Judge not stated in casebook excerpt.] No. Duress is not a complete defense in international law to the killing of innocents. Under the law of some states, duress may be a complete defense to the killing of innocent people. This law, although constituting state practice, is not entitled to the status of customary international law, because this practice is not consistent, especially with many states that apply common law. Moreover, this practice is not supported by *opinio juris,* i.e., those states that do apply this defense do not do so because they believe they are conforming to an international legal obligation. Because there is no consistent state practice or customary law in this area, normative policy considerations, such as social and political policy, are appropriate. The defense relies on cases that have accepted the duress defense where the accused faced death for not killing a victim who inevitably was going to be killed regardless of whether the accused participated. This utilitarian approach is based on the idea that if the victim is going to die anyway, there is no reason the accused should die as it would be unjust for the law to expect the accused to die for nothing. This balancing-of-harms approach is rejected in favor of a clear rule that duress is not a complete defense to those who kill innocent persons. Instead, a mitigation of punishment is the preferred alternative to duress as a complete defense. Mitigation is a more sophisticated and flexible tool for doing justice in individual cases—in some cases where the accused's life is threatened, mitigation can lead to no punishment at all.

DISSENT: (Cassese, J.) Legal constructs and terms of art, such as duress, that originate in national law, cannot be transferred into international criminal proceedings because those proceedings are substantially different from national criminal proceedings and do not reflect the legal paradigms of any one legal system. The Prosecution's contention that customary international law has excluded the common law defense of duress finds minimal support in various national cases, whereas there is copious support for applying the defense. This inconsistency in state practice leads to the conclusion that there is no special rule in customary law as to whether to allow the defense or not. The absence of such a special rule leads to the conclusion—a conclusion the majority does not make—that one should apply, on a case-by-case basis, the general rule of duress to all crimes. One of the elements of this general rule, a requirement that the crime committed was not disproportionate to the evil threatened, will be extremely hard to fulfill where the underlying crime is the killing of innocents, and may never be satisfied where the accused is saving his own life at the expense of his victims. Where the accused may not be able to save the lives of his potential victims regardless of what he does, then duress may succeed as a defense. This is a relevant factor that should be considered in whether to allow the defense. The law in this area must be based on what society can reasonably expect of its members. In certain situations, it may be unreasonable to expect persons under duress not to perpetrate certain offenses. To say, like the majority does, that duress can be used in mitigation, is to ignore that criminal law must determine criminal culpability in the first place. It is also misplaced to resort to policy considerations when international criminal law is ambiguous, since this risks running afoul of the customary principle of *nullum crimen sine lege;* a court must apply law, not policy.

▶ ANALYSIS

Erdemovic (D) was ultimately sentenced to five years in prison. This result may have been more favorable than if the court had applied the duress defense as a complete bar, because that defense requires, as the Dissent points out, a proportionately requirement that is extremely difficult to satisfy in a case such as this, and also requires that the accused did not voluntarily bring about the situation leading to the duress. Ostensibly, this requirement would bar the defense in Erdemovic's (D) case on the ground that he voluntarily joined the Serbian army and knew of its methods and practices. Thus, a rule of mitigation may have served Erdemovic (D) better than an all-or-nothing duress defense.

■═■

Continued on next page.

Quicknotes

DURESS Unlawful threats or other coercive behavior by one person that causes another to commit acts that he would not otherwise do.

MITIGATION Reduction in penalty.

■━■

Prosecutor v. Tadic, Jurisdiction Appeal

Prosecutor (P) v. War criminal (D)

International Criminal Tribunal for the Former Yugoslavia, Appeals Chamber, Case No. IT-94-1-AR72 (1995).

NATURE OF CASE: War crimes trial.

FACT SUMMARY: [Tadic (D), the first defendant to be tried before the International Criminal Tribunal for the Former Yugoslavia (ICTY), challenged, inter alia, the Tribunal's legitimacy.]

🏛 RULE OF LAW
The International Tribunal was lawfully established by the Security Council pursuant to Chapter VII of the Charter of the United Nations as a measure to maintain or restore peace.

FACTS: [The United Nations' Security Council established the International Criminal Tribunal for the Former Yugoslavia (ICTY), which could consider any covered crimes committed in the former Yugoslavia after 1991 (up to the present day). The first defendant to be tried before the ICTY, Tadic (D), challenged, inter alia, the legitimacy of the ICTY, asserting that the Security Council had acted ultra vires in creating the Tribunal.]

ISSUE: Was the International Tribunal lawfully established by the Security Council pursuant to Chapter VII of the Charter of the United Nations as a measure to maintain or restore peace?

HOLDING AND DECISION: [Judge not stated in casebook excerpt.] Yes. The International Tribunal was lawfully established by the Security Council pursuant to Chapter VII of the Charter of the United Nations as a measure to maintain or restore peace. The Security Council plays an important role and exercises wide discretion under Chapter VII to decide on a course of action and evaluate the appropriateness of measures to be taken to restore or maintain peace. The International Tribunal was lawfully established as a measure taken by the Security Council under Chapter VII to restore peace to the former Yugoslavia.

▌ ANALYSIS

Tadic (D) attacked the authority of the Security Council to establish a tribunal for the determination of a criminal charge. Tadic (D) was prosecuted for alleged war crimes committed at a Serb-run concentration camp in Bosnia-Herzegovina, and as part of his legal strategy, argued that creation of the tribunal was beyond the power of the Security Council.

Quicknotes

INTER ALIA Among other things.

ULTRA VIRES Beyond the power.

Azanian People's Organization (AZAPO) and Others v. President of the Republic of South Africa

Apartheid victims (P) v. Government official (D)

[1996] 4 S.A.L.R. 671.

NATURE OF CASE: Proceeding before the South African Constitutional Court to determine the constitutionality of a law for carrying out the Constitution's amnesty provisions.

FACT SUMMARY: [South Africa's post-apartheid Constitution provided for amnesty, and implementing legislation was enacted to carry out these provisions. A group of apartheid victims (P) challenged the law's constitutionality.]

RULE OF LAW
A law that provides for amnesty to those guilty of serious offenses associated with political objectives is not unconstitutional.

FACTS: [South Africa's post-apartheid Constitution provided for amnesty to promote reconciliation and reconstruction. The Promotion of National Unity and Reconciliation Act of 1995 (Act) was enacted to carry out these provisions. The legislation set up the Truth and Reconciliation Commission (TRC), and created three subcommissions—one to investigate the fate of the victims, another to determine indemnification, and the third to administer the amnesty. A group of apartheid victims (P) challenged the law's constitutionality, claiming that Section 20(7) of the Act, providing for immunity from civil or criminal liability for those granted amnesty as well as for the state or organization to which they belonged, was inconsistent with the Constitution's provision for the right to have justiciable disputes settled by a court of law.]

ISSUE: Is a law that provides for amnesty to those guilty of serious offenses associated with political objectives unconstitutional?

HOLDING AND DECISION: [Judge not stated in casebook excerpt.] No. A law that provides for amnesty to those guilty of serious offenses associated with political objectives is not unconstitutional. Amnesty may be granted only where the applicant has made full disclosure and the act or omission for which amnesty is sought was associated with a political objective during the period of apartheid. This provision permits the victims and their survivors to know, what in truth happened through full disclosure by the perpetrators, and provides an incentive for the perpetrators to make full disclosure. The Act thus provides a balance between the need for justice and the need for reconciliation and transition to the future. By providing for amnesty for those guilty of serious offenses and defining the mechanisms through which such amnesty may be secured, the Act does not violate the Constitution. International law in general, and the Geneva Conventions in particular, are relevant to the analysis of the Act's constitutionality only insofar as the Constitution itself should not be presumed to authorize any law that conflicts with the state's international law obligations. As long as an Act of Parliament is not unconstitutional, it can override any contrary rights or obligations under international law. In any event, international law distinguishes between the position of perpetrators of criminal acts in the course of war or similar conflicts between states, and the position of perpetrators of such acts that take place during conflicts that are confined to a single state. With regard to the latter, there is no obligation of the state to prosecute those who might have committed acts that ordinarily would be viewed as human rights violations. Moreover, in the latter situation, international law (e.g., Protocol II to the Geneva Conventions) encourages the granting of amnesty to those who participated in the armed conflict—because all involved inhabit the same territory and must live with each other. Therefore, Section 20(7) does not breach any of the country's obligations under international law, especially since the amnesty granted is not a blanket amnesty.

ANALYSIS

The TRC held numerous hearings throughout South Africa and received testimony from 22,000 victims and witnesses. It received 7,000 applications for amnesty, granted 1,200 of those, and denied 5,500 by the time it closed down in March 2002. However, the government was generally unwilling to fund the reparations recommended by the TRC.

Quicknotes

GENEVA CONVENTION International agreement that governs the conduct of warring nations.

Regina v. Bow Street Metropolitan Stipendiary Magistrate and Others, *Ex Parte* Pinochet Ugarte (No. 3)

Government (P) v. Alleged torturer (D)

[2000] 1 A.C. 147 (1999).

NATURE OF CASE: Appeal of extradition proceedings.

FACT SUMMARY: Pinochet was arrested in London on the basis of a Spanish arrest warrant and held pending extradition to Spain. He claimed that he was not subject to any legal proceeding in London because of his immunity as a former head of state.

🏛 RULE OF LAW
Although international law grants state immunity to the international crime of torture, a state that ratified the Torture Convention is not entitled to claim such immunity.

FACTS: In 1998, Pinochet visited London for treatment of a back ailment. Spanish magistrates handling a case against Pinochet in Spain asked Scotland Yard to detain him. Subsequently, Spain issued an arrest warrant for Pinochet. Pinochet was arrested by detectives from Scotland Yard and Spain then requested Pinochet's extradition. Pinochet argued that as a former head of state he was immune from legal process in Britain.

ISSUE: Although international law grants state immunity to the international crime of torture, is a state that ratified the Torture Convention entitled to claim such immunity?

HOLDING AND DECISION: (Lord Browne-Wilkinson) No. Although international law grants state immunity to the international crime of torture, a state that ratified the Torture Convention is not entitled to claim such immunity. While international law grants state immunity in relation to the international crime of torture, a state can waive such immunity. Here, Chile is not entitled to claim such immunity since Chile, Spain, and the United Kingdom are all parties to the Torture Convention. The obligations that Chile undertook by being a party to the Convention override any claim of immunity, and, therefore, any claims to immunity by Chile were lost when Chile ratified the Convention. Torture is considered a crime against humanity and an individual can be prosecuted personally under international law for such an international crime. Moreover, the international law prohibiting torture enables states to take universal jurisdiction over it wherever it is committed. Although local courts could take jurisdiction, prior to the Torture Convention there was no tribunal or court in which to try international crimes of torture. The Torture Convention was thus established to provide an international system under which the international criminal could find no safe haven. Parties to the Torture Convention are bound to give effect to its provisions. It is a basic principle of international law

that states, heads of state, and diplomatic representatives all enjoy criminal immunity from prosecution in the forum state. An ex-ambassador retains immunity only for official acts during his tenure in post. An ex-head of state cannot also be sued in respect of acts performed while head of state. An essential feature of the international crime of torture, however, is that it must be committed by or with the acquiescence of a public official or other person acting in an official capacity. As a result, the defendants in torture cases will be officials yet, as former heads of state, they will be immune from prosecution. This cannot be the intent of the Torture Convention. There can thus be no case outside of Chile in which a successful prosecution for torture can be brought unless Chile is prepared to waive its officials' immunity.

SEPARATE OPINION: (Lord Goff) Any waiver of its immunity by Chile must be express. It is argued that since torture contrary to the Convention can only be committed by a public official or one acting in an official capacity, and since it is in respect of these acts that states can assert immunity, it would be inconsistent with states' obligations under the Convention for them to be able to invoke immunity in cases of torture that are contrary to the Convention. However, there is no doubt that before the Convention a state could assert immunity for torture by one acting in an official capacity, and because there is no express provision in the Convention excluding such immunity, the immunity must be implied in the Convention. Chile is correct in asserting that waiver of such immunity must always be express, and, therefore, the argument that such waiver may be circumvented on the basis that, for the purposes of the Convention, such torture does not form part of the functions of those acting in an official capacity—including heads of state—must be rejected. Any limitations placed on governmental functions, such as those of a head of state, to exclude them from acts of torture covered by the Convention would have to be implied from the Convention itself, as there was no express limitation set forth therein. However, to imply such terms in a treaty, except in the most obvious cases, is inadvisable. Here, there was nothing in the negotiating history of the Convention or the travaux preparatoires that reveals that any consideration was given to waiver of state immunity. Because the Convention's express text does not reflect that the parties thereto reached agreement on this issue, it should not be implied.

SEPARATE OPINION: (Lord Hope) The Torture Convention does not contain any provision that deals

Continued on next page.

expressly with the question of whether heads of state or former heads of state are or are not to have immunity from allegations that they have committed torture and such intent should not be implied. The allegations against Pinochet amount to an international crime, a crime against humanity because it was committed as part of a widespread attack against a civilian population on national, political, and ethnic grounds. The Torture Convention, which enabled jurisdiction over such crimes to be exercised in the courts of a foreign state, was in place at the time he committed these crimes, and, therefore, it was no longer open to any state that was a signatory to the convention to invoke immunity in the event of widespread torture after that date. This is, therefore, not a case of waiver nor should such a waiver be implied. The obligations Chile undertook by being a party to the Convention override any claim of immunity and therefore any claims to immunity were lost when Chile ratified the Convention.

▶ ANALYSIS

As the opinion notes, although the Court found that Pinochet was not immune from prosecution because of his status as a former head of state, the Lords had different views as to why that was the case. Furthermore, it was subsequently determined that Pinochet lacked the mental capacity to stand trial and he was allowed to return to Chile. After his return, Chile stripped him of his immunity and prosecuted him for kidnapping. An appeals court later ruled, however, that he suffered from dementia and was therefore precluded from prosecution.

■■■

Quicknotes

EXTRADITION   The surrender by one state or nation to another of an individual allegedly guilty of committing a crime in that area.

IMMUNITY   Exemption from a legal obligation.

■■■

Case Concerning the Arrest Warrant of 11 April 2000
(Democratic Republic of the Congo v. Belgium)

Sovereign nation (P) v. Sovereign nation (D)

2002 I.C.J. 121 (Feb. 14).

NATURE OF CASE: Proceeding before the International Court of Justice (ICJ) to determine if an incumbent diplomat enjoys immunity from arrest.

FACT SUMMARY: Belgium (D) issued an arrest warrant for the Minister for Foreign Affairs of the Democratic Republic of the Congo (DRC) (P). DRC (P) sued, claiming that Belgium (D) had violated the diplomatic immunity enjoyed by its Minister.

> ## 🏛 RULE OF LAW
> The issuance by a state of an arrest warrant for an incumbent Minister for Foreign Affairs of another state violates the Minister's diplomatic immunity.

FACTS: Belgium (D) issued an arrest warrant for DRC's (P) Minister for Foreign Affairs, Abdoulaye Yerodia Ndombasi (Yerodia), for crimes against humanity and war crimes he allegedly committed as an advisor to DRC's (P) president during its civil war. The DRC (P) claimed, among other things, that the warrant violated Yerodia's diplomatic immunity.

ISSUE: Does the issuance by a state of an arrest warrant for an incumbent Minister for Foreign Affairs of another state violate the Minister's diplomatic immunity?

HOLDING AND DECISION: [Judge not stated in casebook excerpt.] Yes. The issuance by a state of an arrest warrant for an incumbent Minister for Foreign Affairs of another state violates the Minister's diplomatic immunity. Ministers for Foreign Affairs are granted diplomatic immunity under customary international law. When he is abroad a Minister enjoys full immunity from criminal jurisdiction and inviolability. There is no exception to this immunity under customary international law for Ministers suspected of having committed war crimes or crimes against humanity, nor is there such an exception in the legal instruments creating international criminal tribunals. This jurisdictional immunity, however, does not mean impunity—even a Minister is not exonerated from all criminal responsibility. Therefore, an incumbent (or former) Minister may be prosecuted in his own country or if his own country waives immunity. A former Minister may be prosecuted for crimes committed before or after they hold office, or for acts while serving as Minister that were committed in a private capacity. Also, special international tribunals may have jurisdiction to prosecute Ministers for certain crimes. The mere issuance by Belgium (D) of the arrest warrant, which fully authorized arrest, was itself a violation of Yerodia's diplomatic immunity

and, by extension, constituted a violation of an obligation of Belgium (D) toward the DRC (P).

▶ ANALYSIS

The ICJ's remedy was to order Belgium (D) to cancel the warrant and inform all law enforcement authorities of this cancellation.

Quicknotes

IMMUNITY Exemption from a legal obligation.

The Law of the Sea

Quick Reference Rules of Law

The Corfu Channel Case (United Kingdom v. Albania)

Warships (P) v. Territorial waters (D)

1949 I.C.J. 4 (Apr. 9).

NATURE OF CASE: Proceeding before the International Court of Justice.

FACT SUMMARY: The U.K. (P) claimed that it had a right to send its warships through straits used for international navigation.

RULE OF LAW
The test of whether a channel should be considered as belonging to the class of international highways through which passage cannot be prohibited by a coastal state in time of peace is its geographical situation connecting two parts of the high seas and not the fact of its being used for international navigation.

FACTS: British warships (P) sailing through the North Corfu Channel were fired on by Albanian (D) forces. The U.K. (P) protested to the Albanian (D) government which asserted that foreign ships had no right to pass through Albanian territorial waters without prior notification to, and the permission of, Albanian authorities. The U.K. (P) claimed that in time of peace states can send their ships for innocent purposes through straits used for international navigation. Albania (D) claimed this channel did not belong to the class of international highways through which a right of passage exists because it was used almost exclusively for local traffic. That channel had also been in dispute because Greece and Albania had both claimed bordering territory and Albania was afraid of Greek incursions.

ISSUE: Is the test of whether a channel should be considered as belonging to the class of international highways through which passage cannot be prohibited by a coastal state in time of peace its geographical situation connecting two parts of the high seas and not the fact of its being used for international navigation?

HOLDING AND DECISION: [Judge not stated in casebook excerpt.] Yes. The test of whether a channel should be considered as belonging to the class of international highways through which passage cannot be prohibited by a coastal state in time of peace is its geographical situation connecting two parts of the high seas and not the fact of its being used for international navigation. The North Corfu Channel should be considered as belonging to the class of international highways through which passage cannot be prohibited by a coastal state in time of peace. In light of the state of war with Greece, Albania (D) would have been justified in issuing regulations in respect of the passage of warships through the strait, but not in prohibiting such passage. The United Kingdom authorities did not violate Albania's sovereignty.

▶ ANALYSIS

The U.N. Convention on the Law of the Sea was passed in 1982. It provides that all states, whether coastal or landlocked, enjoy the right of innocent passage through the territorial sea. The territorial sea was held to exist up to a limit not exceeding 12 nautical miles from the coast.

■==■

Quicknotes

TERRITORIAL SEA That portion of the sea that is three miles off a nation's coast and over which that nation has jurisdiction.

■==■

Fisheries Jurisdiction Case (United Kingdom v. Iceland)

Fishing nation (P) v. Fishing nation (D)

1974 I.C.J. 3 (July 25).

NATURE OF CASE: Proceeding before the International Court of Justice (ICJ) to determine validity of extension of fisheries zone.

FACT SUMMARY: Iceland (D) extended its fisheries zone from 12 to 50 miles. The United Kingdom (U.K.) (P) challenged the extension as unlawful.

RULE OF LAW
All states exercising fishing rights must pay reasonable regard to the interests of other states.

FACTS: In 1961, the U.K. (P) and Iceland (D) concluded an exchange of notes whereby the U.K. (P) recognized Iceland's 12-mile fisheries zone, and Iceland (D) agreed periodically to allow U.K. (P) vessels in some areas within 12 miles for three years and to notify the U.K. (P) of any increases in the zone. In 1972, Iceland (D) announced that it would extend its fisheries jurisdiction to 50 miles and issued regulations (the Icelandic Regulations of 14 July 1972) to effect this change. The U.K. (P) challenged this extension as unlawful and asked the ICJ to resolve the dispute.

ISSUE: Must all states exercising fishing rights pay reasonable regard to the interests of other states?

HOLDING AND DECISION: [Judge not stated in casebook excerpt.] Yes. All states exercising fishing rights must pay reasonable regard to the interests of other states. Thus, Iceland (D) is prohibited from excluding U.K. (P) vessels beyond Iceland's 12-mile fisheries zone. The practice of using a fishery zone and extending that zone to 12 miles from a state's baseline is part of customary law, as is the concept of preferential rights for coastal states who are dependent on their fisheries. The U.K. (P) has expressly recognized Iceland's preferential rights in the disputed waters, but has also invoked its own historic fishing rights in those waters on the ground that the coastal state must give reasonable regard to such rights. State practice requires that a coastal state's preferential rights be negotiated. Iceland's (D) unilateral extension of its fisheries zone is a claim of exclusive rights, which goes beyond its preferential rights, which are not compatible with the exclusion of all fishing by other states. The coastal state must take into account the position of other states, particularly when those other states have established economic dependence on the same fishing grounds—as the U.K. (P) has in this case by showing that her fishing industry would be adversely affected by being excluded from those waters. For these reasons, as a matter of law, Iceland is not entitled unilaterally to exclude U.K. (P) vessels beyond the 12-mile zone agreed to in the Exchange of Notes. However, because Iceland (D) has preferential rights in the waters beyond the 12-mile zone, and the U.K. (P) has historic rights in those waters as well, the two states are obligated to recognize each other's rights, and to negotiate an agreement on the basis of such recognition.

ANALYSIS

In 1975, Iceland again extended its fisheries zone from 50 miles to 200 miles, defying the ICJ's ruling. Because of Iceland's important role in the North Atlantic Treaty Organization (NATO), Iceland had enough leverage to enforce this zone, and most foreign fishing vessels are now excluded from Iceland's 200-mile zone—demonstrating the practical limitations on the ICJ's power.

North Sea Continental Shelf Cases (Federal Republic of Germany/ Denmark and Netherlands)

Denmark (P) and the Netherlands (P) v. Germany (D)

1969 I.C.J. 3 (1969).

NATURE OF CASE: Action to determine national boundaries.

FACT SUMMARY: Denmark (P) and the Netherlands (P) contended that customary rules of international law determined the boundaries of areas located on the continental shelf between those countries and the Federal Republic of Germany (D).

🏛 RULE OF LAW
A custom, to be binding as international law, must amount to a settled practice and must be rendered obligatory by a rule of law requiring it.

FACTS: Denmark (P) and the Netherlands (P) contended that the boundaries between their respective areas of the continental shelf in the North Sea, and the area claimed by the Federal Republic of Germany (D), should be determined by the application of the principle of equidistance set forth in Article 6 of the Geneva Convention of 1958 on the Continental Shelf, which by January 1, 1969 had been ratified or acceded to by 39 states, but to which Germany (D) was not a party. Denmark (P) and the Netherlands (P) contended that Germany (D) was bound to accept delimitation on an equidistance basis, because the use of this method was not merely a conventional obligation, but was a rule which was part of the corpus of general international law, and like other rules of general or customary international law, was binding automatically on Germany (D), independent of any specific assent, direct or indirect, given by Germany (D).

ISSUE: Must a custom, in order to be binding as international law, amount to a settled practice which is rendered obligatory by a rule of law requiring it?

HOLDING AND DECISION: [Judge not stated in casebook excerpt.] Yes. A custom, to be binding as international law, must amount to a settled practice and must be rendered obligatory by a rule of law requiring it. The equidistance principle, as stated in Article 6 of the Geneva Convention, is not part of customary international law. Article 6 is of the type of articles under which reservations may be made by any state on signing or ratifying the Convention, so that the state is not necessarily bound in all instances by that article. A general or customary law has equal force for all members of the international community and cannot be unilaterally abrogated. Article 6 has not been accepted as part of the general corpus of international law by the *opinio juris*, so as to have become binding even for countries which have never and do not become parties to

the Convention. Rather than giving the principle of equidistance a fundamental norm-creating character, which is necessary to the formation of a general rule of law, Article 6 makes the obligation to use the equidistance method a secondary one, which comes into play only in the absence of an agreement between the parties. In order for a rule to constitute the *opinio juris*, two conditions must be fulfilled. Not only must the acts concerned amount to a settled practice, but they must also be such, or be carried out in such a way, as to be evidence of a belief that this practice is rendered obligatory by the existence of a rule of law requiring it. Accordingly, judgment is rendered for Germany (D).

DISSENT: (Tanaka, J.) The equitable principle requires only that the parties consider diverse and vague principles that may never result in agreement. The Court did not provide any indication as to what are the principles and rules of international law that apply to the negotiations. The parties should have the option of ending negotiations and applying instead the equidistance principle.

SEPARATE OPINION: (Jessup, J.) The reason the parties are concerned with the delimitation of their respective portions is the probable existence of oil and gas in the seabed. The exploitation of the oil and gas resources of the continental shelf of the North Sea was foremost on the minds of the parties, but none of them was prepared to base its case on consideration of this factor.

▶ ANALYSIS

Justice Lachs's analysis of the concept of *opinio juris* is in accord with the position taken by some legal scholars who maintain that *opinio juris* may be presumed from uniformities of practice regarding matters viewed normally as involving legal rights and obligations. A contrary position maintains that the practice of states must be accompanied by or consist of statements that something is law before it can become law.

■=■

Protecting the International Environment

Quick Reference Rules of Law

Lac Lanoux Arbitration (Spain v. France)

Downstream user (D) v. Upstream user (P)

24 I.L.R. 101 (1956).

NATURE OF CASE: Arbitration of breach of treaty.

FACT SUMMARY: The French government (P) proposed a plan to use Lac Lanoux for hydroelectric purposes to which Spain (D) objected.

🏛 RULE OF LAW
States do not need the prior agreement of interested states to use the hydraulic power of international waterways.

FACTS: France (P) proposed a plan to exploit the hydraulic power of Lac Lanoux. The plan would affect the flow of water in Spain (D). Spain (D) protested the French proposal on the ground that any French plan must be based on agreement between the two countries. The parties submitted the question to international arbitration.

ISSUE: Do states need the prior agreement of interested states to use the hydraulic power of international waterways?

HOLDING AND DECISION: [Judge not stated in casebook excerpt.] No. States do not need the prior agreement of interested states to use the hydraulic power of international waterways. The ability of an upstream user to utilize its territorial waters is vital to that state's sovereignty. International law cannot require a state to enter an agreement prior to using its own resources. However, there is a good faith obligation on the part of the upstream user to take into account the interests of the downstream user. In this case, France (P) has offered to pay full restitution for diversion of water normally flowing into Spain (D). France (P) has adequately attempted to safeguard Spain's (D) interests and sufficiently involved Spain (D) in the preparations of its project.

▶ ANALYSIS

Although international environmental law comprises elements of existing international law, such as rules of sovereignty and territorial integrity, new approaches are evolving to deal with issues of transboundary pollution. One rule holds that no state has the right to use or permit the use of its territory in such a manner as to cause injury to the territory of another. This is the rule of strict liability imposed in the *Trail Smelter Arbitration (United States v. Canada)*, Arbitral Trib., 3 U.N. Rep. Int'l Arb. Awards 1905 (1941). Of course, this position directly conflicts with international judicial reluctance to impair the territorial sovereignty of a state.

Quicknotes

ARBITRATION An agreement to have a dispute heard and decided by a neutral third party, rather than through legal proceedings.

WATER RIGHTS The right to reduce water naturally flowing to possession for private use.

Case Concerning the Gabcikovo-Nagymaros Project (Hungary/Slovakia)

Treaty partner (P) v. Treaty partner (D)

1997 I.C.J. 7.

NATURE OF CASE: Action before the International Court of Justice regarding a violation of a Treaty between Hungary and Slovakia.

FACT SUMMARY: [Hungary abandoned work relating to the Gabcikovo-Nagymaros Project claiming a state of ecological necessity defense. Czechoslovakia (present day Slovakia) continued work on the project but diverted most of the Danube River away from Hungary. Both states claimed that a violation of a Treaty between the two had occurred.]

🏛 RULE OF LAW

(1) A state of ecological necessity does not justify the breach of a treaty where the alleged ecological perils are not established or imminent and the breaching state could have responded to the perceived perils in ways other than by breaching the treaty.

(2) It is an international wrongful act to divert an international watercourse away from a state without its consent.

FACTS: [Hungary and Czechoslovakia had a 1977 Treaty to build a series of dams on the Danube River. The Treaty provided for the construction of two series of locks at Gabcikovo, Czechoslovakia, and Nagymaros, Hungary, which together were to constitute a single operational system of works financed, constructed, operated, and owned by both states. In 1989, Hungary suspended construction of the Nagymaros dam and in 1992 sought to terminate the treaty. In response, Czechoslovakia continued work on the project under a revised plan whereby the dam was built entirely on Czech soil, but diverted most of the Danube River away from Hungary.] To justify its conduct, Hungary relied on a "state of ecological necessity." Hungary argued that the various installations of the Gabcikovo-Nagymaros System of Locks had been designed to enable the Gabcikovo power plant to operate in a manner that carried unacceptable ecological risks. Hungary further argued that had the Nagymaros dam been built, the water supply to Budapest would have been diminished and aquatic habitats threatened. The states agreed to have their dispute resolved by the ICJ, which evaluated the existence of a state of necessity in light of Article 33 of the Draft Articles on the International Responsibility of States.

ISSUE:

(1) Does a state of ecological necessity justify the breach of a treaty where the alleged ecological perils are not established or imminent and the breaching state could have responded to the perceived perils in ways other than by breaching the treaty?

(2) Is it an international wrongful act to divert an international watercourse away from a state without its consent?

HOLDING AND DECISION: [Judge not stated in casebook excerpt.]

(1) No. A state of ecological necessity does not justify the breach of a treaty where the alleged ecological perils are not established or imminent and the breaching state could have responded to the perceived perils in ways other than by breaching the treaty. Hungary's claim of ecological necessity was not justified because the claimed perils were not established nor were they imminent and Hungary could have responded to these perils in ways other than abandoning the work for which it had been entrusted. A state of necessity can only be accepted on an exceptional basis. The concerns expressed by Hungary for its natural environment in the region affected by the Gabcikovo-Nagymaros Project related to an essential interest of that state as described in Article 33. A grave danger to the ecological preservation of all or some of the territory of a state could occasion a necessity. In regard to Nagymaros however, any grave peril for the environment in the area that may have existed was uncertain and not imminent when work on the dam was abandoned. In regard to Gabcikovo, the peril described by Hungary was also uncertain. Hungary could also have resorted to other means in order to respond to the dangers that it apprehended.

(2) Yes. It is an international wrongful act to divert an international watercourse away from a state without its consent. Czechoslovakia should not be allowed to divert the river away from Hungary. Czechoslovakia was not entitled to divert the Danube River because it is a shared international watercourse and international boundary river. Although Hungary had agreed to the damming of the river and the diversion of its waters, it was only in the context of joint operation and a sharing of its benefits that Hungary had given its consent. The suspension and withdrawal of that consent constituted a violation of Hungary's legal obligations, but that does not mean that Hungary forfeited its basic right to an equitable and reasonable sharing of the resources of an international watercourse. Czechoslovakia's actions violated certain provisions of the Treaty and constituted an international wrongful act. In addition, Czechoslovakia's

Continued on next page.

actions were not a justified countermeasure in response to Hungary's breach of the Treaty because they were not commensurate with the injury suffered. Czechoslovakia, by unilaterally assuming control of a shared resource, deprived Hungary of its right to an equitable and reasonable share of the natural resources of the Danube and thus failed to respect Hungary's proportionality, which is required by international law.

▶ *ANALYSIS*

The court also considered other issues and made several rulings. The court indicated that newly developed norms of environmental law were relevant for the implementation of the Treaty and could be incorporated therein. To evaluate the project's environmental risks, the court indicated that current environmental standards should be taken into consideration. The court also ruled that the 1977 Agreement was still in force and ordered the parties to recreate a joint regime. Finally, the court held that the consequences of the wrongful acts of both parties would be wiped out if they resumed their cooperation in the utilization of the shared water resources of the Danube and if the multi-purpose program in the form of a coordinated single unit for the use development and protection of the watercourse was implemented in equitable and reasonable manner.

■■■

Southern Bluefin Tuna Cases (New Zealand and Australia v. Japan)

Fishing nations (P) v. Fishing nation (D)

Int'l. Trib. L. Sea (27 August 1999).

NATURE OF CASE: Proceeding before the International Tribunal for the Law of the Sea (ITLOS) for provisional measures under the United Nations Convention on the Law of the Sea (UNCLOS).

FACT SUMMARY: [Japan (D) started an experimental program to fish for Southern Bluefin Tuna (SBT). Australia and New Zealand (P) sought provisional measures, claiming that Japan's (D) program violated provisions of UNCLOS and, by endangering SBT, the precautionary principle.]

> ### RULE OF LAW
> Where states have agreed to conserve a certain fish species but cannot agree on the scientific implications of an experimental fishing program engaged in unilaterally by one of the states, all parties are obligated to take precautions to ensure the effective conservation of that species.

FACTS: [Australia (P), New Zealand (P), and Japan (D) had entered the Convention for the Conservation of Southern Bluefin Tuna (CSBT Convention), which established a commission that on an annual basis set the total catch of SBT that each party was allowed. Although the parties discussed creating an experimental fishing program to enhance their understanding of SBT stock, they were unable to come to agreement on such a program. In 1998, Japan (D) started unilaterally such a program, a result of which was that Japan's taking of SBT exceeded its 1997 allocation (no levels had been set in 1998 or 1999). In 1999, Australia (P) and New Zealand (P) instituted arbitral proceedings against Japan (D), and, pending constitution of the arbitral tribunal, sought provisional measures from the ITLOS, claiming that the situation was an urgent one that would cause immediate harm to their rights and to the marine environment. The parties agreed that the stock of SBT was severely depleted and at its historically lowest levels.] Accordingly, Australia (P) and New Zealand (P) claimed that Japan's (D) program violated provisions of UNCLOS and, by endangering SBT, the precautionary principle.

ISSUE: Where states have agreed to conserve a certain fish species but cannot agree on the scientific implications of an experimental fishing program engaged in unilaterally by one of the states, are all parties obligated to take precautions to ensure the effective conservation of that species?

HOLDING AND DECISION: [Judge not stated in casebook excerpt.] Yes. Where states have agreed to conserve a certain fish species but cannot agree on the scientific implications of an experimental fishing program engaged in unilaterally by one of the states, all parties are

obligated to take precautions to ensure the effective conservation of that species. Japan (D) contends that the scientific evidence shows that its fishing program will do no further harm to SBT stock. Australia and New Zealand (P) claim that the scientific evidence shows that Japan's (D) program could endanger the existence of SBT. Given that the parties should act with "prudence and caution" to ensure the conservation of SBT stock, and given the lack of agreement by the parties on the scientific evidence, both as how to conserve SBT and as to whether their conservation efforts have so far been effective, the parties must ensure, unless they agree otherwise, that their catches of SBT do not exceed the last allowable level, and, in calculating their catch, must include any catch made as part of an experimental fishing program. Also, none of the party members shall conduct an experimental fishing program without the agreement of the other parties, or unless the experimental catch is counted against its annual national allocation.

SEPARATE OPINION: (Laing, J.) Australia (P) and New Zealand (P) base their requests for provisional measures largely on the precautionary principle of international law. This principle requires states to be cautious when making decisions about actions that entail threats to the environment while there is scientific uncertainty about the effect of such actions. Its main thesis is that absolute proof should not be necessary before steps are taken to minimize potential risks. Its legal effect is to shift the burden of proof to the state in control of the territory from which the harm might emanate or to the responsible party. Although it seems that this principle is increasingly being accepted, the consequence of its application in specific situations is not clear. Accordingly, it is not possible to determine whether customary international law recognizes a precautionary principle. It is, nevertheless, clear that the UNCLOS takes a precautionary approach, and here, the majority has also taken such an approach in issuing its provisional measures. Adopting a precautionary approach provides greater flexibility than adopting a precautionary principle, given the policy dilemmas posed by scientific uncertainty.

ANALYSIS

Some of the specifics of the precautionary principle that remain unresolved are: the level and type of harm that triggers the principle; whether financial limitations, or cost-benefit considerations, limit the measures required to be taken in response to a potential risk; and whether possible health risks emanating from the very remedies designed to avoid environmental risks need to be factored in. Another concern

Continued on next page.

about the principle is that it is too imprecise and subjective a notion.

▪══▪

Quicknotes

BURDEN OF PROOF The duty of a party to introduce evidence to support a fact that is in dispute in an action.

▪══▪

CHAPTER 12

Managing the World Economy

Quick Reference Rules of Law

LG & E Energy Corporation v. Argentine Republic

U.S. company (P) v Foreign nation (D)

International Centre for the Settlement of Investment Disputes, ICSID Case No. ARB/02/1 (Oct. 3, 2006).

NATURE OF CASE: Arbitral case brought under bilateral investment treaty (BIT).

FACT SUMMARY: [LG & E Energy Corporation (LG & E) (P), a U.S. investor in Argentina's (D) gas sector, contended that Argentina's response to that country's economic crisis, which had the effect of drastically reducing the value of LG & E's (P) investment, violated the U.S.-Argentina BIT and was tantamount to an expropriation.]

🏛 RULE OF LAW

A state measure is not equivalent to expropriation where it does not effect a permanent or severe deprivation of an investor's rights in an investment.

FACTS: [In response to a severe economic crisis, Argentina (D) implemented various emergency measures in an attempt to stabilize its economy. One of these measures was the so-called Emergency Law, which abolished peso-dollar convertibility, so that the one-to-one peg of the peso to the dollar no longer existed. In addition, the law terminated the right of privatized utilities, including the gas companies, to payments calculated in dollars and the right to adjust those tariffs on the basis of the U.S. producer price index (PPI). The law forbade public utility companies from suspending or modifying compliance with their obligations under their concessions and licenses. The Emergency Law provided for a process of renegotiation of licenses to operate the gas transportation and distribution companies. Several attempts by the gas companies and the Government (D) to implement emergency increases in gas and electricity tariffs were blocked by the Argentine (D) courts. Foreign investors claimed that the Government's (D) measures produced devastating consequences for their investments. Some claimed, for example, that the sudden devaluation of the peso reduced their revenue by two-thirds. Firms in the gas sector asserted that revenues from tariffs fell by nearly 75 percent and that the value of their stock shares fell by more than 90 percent. In response, Argentina (D) argued that any losses resulted from the firms' business decisions. One U.S. investor, LG & E (P), brought an arbitral action against Argentina (D), asserting that the Emergency Law violated the U.S.-Argentina bilateral investment treaty. One issue was whether Argentina's (D) actions were tantamount, or equivalent to, expropriation.]

ISSUE: Is a state measure equivalent to expropriation where it does not effect a permanent or severe deprivation of an investor's rights in an investment?

HOLDING AND DECISION: [Judge not stated in casebook excerpt.] No. A state measure is not equivalent to expropriation where it does not effect a permanent or severe deprivation of an investor's rights in an investment. A state's actions are "equivalent to expropriation" or "tantamount to expropriation" where they are not an overt taking but effectively neutralize the benefit of the foreign investor's property by removing the investor's control over the investment or its ability to manage day-to-day operations. To evaluate whether an expropriation has occurred the degree to which the state's action interferes with the investor's rights must be balanced against the state's power to adopt its policies. To determine the degree of interference with the investor's ownership rights, the measure's interference with the investor's reasonable expectations and the measure's duration must be analyzed. In most cases, interference with the investment's ability to carry on its business is not satisfied where the investment continues to operate, notwithstanding diminished profits, and the interference is not permanent. It is also necessary to distinguish between the state's right to adopt policies for the social or general welfare and policies that are expropriatory. Where the measure is enacted for the social or general welfare, the state will not be liable except where the measure is obviously disproportionate to the need being addressed. Here, although the Argentina (D) adopted severe measures that clearly impacted LG & E's (P) investment, those measures did not deprive LG & E (P) of the right to enjoy its investment, which it continued to own. In fact, that ownership interest has rebounded in value since the economic crisis. Additionally, LG & E (P) did not lose control over its shares in its gas sector investments and was not deprived of managerial control. Thus, without a permanent, severe deprivation of LG&E's (P) rights with regard to its investment, or almost complete deprivation of the value of LG&E's (P) investment, the emergency measures did not constitute expropriation.

▶ ANALYSIS

Indirect expropriation may show itself in a gradual or growing form—creeping expropriation—or through a sole and unique action—de facto expropriation.

Quicknotes

ARBITRATION An alternative resolution process where a dispute is heard and decided by a neutral third party, rather than through legal proceedings.

Enron Corp. v. Argentine Republic

U.S. company (P) v. Foreign nation (D)

International Centre for the Settlement of Investment Disputes, ICSID Case No. ARB/01/3 (May 22, 2007).

NATURE OF CASE: Arbitral case brought under bilateral investment treaty (BIT).

FACT SUMMARY: [Enron Corp. (P), a U.S. investor in Argentina's (D) gas sector, contended that Argentina's response to that country's economic crisis, which had the effect of drastically reducing the value of Enron's (P) investment, violated the U.S.-Argentina BIT.]

🏛 RULE OF LAW
A bilateral investment treaty's requirement of fair and equitable treatment of investors is breached where a state's actions have caused destabilization of the legal and business framework for investment and have undermined investors' reasonable expectations by failing to maintain conditions relied on by investors when making their initial investment.

FACTS: [In response to a severe economic crisis, Argentina (D) implemented various emergency measures in an attempt to stabilize its economy. One of these measures was the so-called Emergency Law, which abolished peso-dollar convertibility, so that the one-to-one peg of the peso to the dollar no longer existed. In addition, the law terminated the right of privatized utilities, including the gas companies, to payments calculated in dollars and the right to adjust those tariffs on the basis of the U.S. producer price index (PPI). The law forbade public utility companies from suspending or modifying compliance with their obligations under their concessions and licenses. The Emergency Law provided for a process of renegotiation of licenses to operate the gas transportation and distribution companies. Several attempts by the gas companies and the Government (D) to implement emergency increases in gas and electricity tariffs were blocked by the Argentine (D) courts. Foreign investors claimed that the Government's (D) measures produced devastating consequences for their investments. Some claimed, for example, that the sudden devaluation of the peso reduced their revenue by two-thirds. Firms in the gas sector asserted that revenues from tariffs fell by nearly 75 percent and that the value of their stock shares fell by more than 90 percent. In response, Argentina (D) argued that any losses resulted from the firms' business decisions. One U.S. investor, Enron Corp. (P), brought an arbitral action against Argentina (D), asserting that the Emergency Law violated the U.S.-Argentina bilateral investment treaty. One issue was whether Argentina's (D) actions failed to afford Enron (P) fair and equitable treatment.]

ISSUE: Is a bilateral investment treaty's requirement of fair and equitable treatment of investors breached where a state's actions have caused destabilization of the legal and business framework for investment and have undermined

investors' reasonable expectations by failing to maintain conditions relied on by investors when making their initial investment?

HOLDING AND DECISION: [Judge not stated in casebook excerpt.] Yes. A bilateral investment treaty's requirement of fair and equitable treatment of investors is breached where a state's actions have caused destabilization of the legal and business framework for investment and have undermined investors' reasonable expectations by failing to maintain conditions relied on by investors when making their initial investment. The treaty's preamble links the fair and equitable standard to maintaining a stable legal and business framework for investing. While the maintenance of such a stable framework does not require the freezing of the legal system or elimination of the Government's (D) regulatory power, it does require maintaining the framework to such a degree that there are no adverse legal effects on investing. Investors' expectations, which were based on conditions existing at the time the investment was made and on which the investor relied, must be honored. Here, Argentina's (D) actions have beyond any doubt changed the legal and business framework under which Enron's (P) investment was decided and implemented. Argentina (D) guaranteed that tariffs would be calculated in U.S. dollars, converted into pesos for billing purposes, adjusted semi-annually in accordance with the U.S. PPI and sufficient to cover costs and a reasonable rate of return. Argentina's (D) emergency measures dismantled those guarantees, causing investment uncertainty and instability. Thus, a stable legal framework that initially induced investment is no longer in place and has been missing for several years. Accordingly, there was an objective breach of the fair and equitable treatment due under the treaty.

▶ ANALYSIS

The fair and equitable standard has been evolving. Under traditional international law, disputes over whether a host state afforded investors fair and equitable treatment were rare. Today, in contrast, it is one of the most commonly disputed standards—and one under which investors succeed in a significant number of cases. Moreover, the standard can require treatment beyond that available in customary law.

■━■

Quicknotes

ARBITRATION An alternative resolution process where a dispute is heard and decided by a neutral third party, rather than through legal proceedings.

■━■

LG & E Energy Corporation v. Argentine Republic

U.S. company (P) v Foreign nation (D)

International Centre for the Settlement of Investment Disputes, ICSID Case No. ARB/02/1 (Oct. 3, 2006).

NATURE OF CASE: Arbitral case brought under bilateral investment treaty (BIT).

FACT SUMMARY: [After Argentina (D) was found to have violated the U.S.-Argentina BIT based on its response to Argentina's (D) severe economic crisis, which response had the effect of drastically reducing the value of foreign investors' investments, Argentina (D) argued that its liability was excused by the BIT and by the customary international law doctrine of necessity.]

> ## 🏛 RULE OF LAW
> A state's violation of a bilateral investment treaty is excused under the doctrine of necessity and by the need to maintain public order or to protect its security interests where its economy, society and political system are in a state of emergency such that the state's survival is threatened.

FACTS: [In response to a severe economic crisis, Argentina (D) implemented various emergency measures in an attempt to stabilize its economy and prevent a state of anarchy and political and social upheaval and chaos. One of these measures was the so-called Emergency Law, which abolished peso-dollar convertibility, so that the one-to-one peg of the peso to the dollar no longer existed. In addition, the law terminated the right of privatized utilities, including gas companies, to payments calculated in dollars and the right to adjust those tariffs on the basis of the U.S. producer price index (PPI). The law forbade public utility companies from suspending or modifying compliance with their obligations under their concessions and licenses. The Emergency Law provided for a process of renegotiation of licenses to operate the gas transportation and distribution companies. Several attempts by the gas companies and the Government (D) to implement emergency increases in gas and electricity tariffs were blocked by the Argentine (D) courts. Some U.S. investors (P) brought arbitral cases, claiming that the Government's (D) measures produced devastating consequences for their investments and violated the U.S.-Argentina BIT. After Argentina (D) was found to have breached the BIT, Argentina (D) argued that its liability was excused by the customary international law doctrine of necessity as well as by the BIT itself, which provided that parties would not be precluded from applying measures necessary for the maintenance of public order and the protection of their security interests.]

ISSUE: Is a state's violation of a bilateral investment treaty excused under the doctrine of necessity and by the need to maintain public order or to protect its security interests where its economy, society and political system are in a state of emergency such that the state's survival is threatened?

HOLDING AND DECISION: [Judge not stated in casebook excerpt.] Yes. A state's violation of a bilateral investment treaty is excused under the doctrine of necessity and by the need to maintain public order or to protect its security interests where its economy, society and political system are in a state of emergency such that the state's survival is threatened. The evidence shows that the conditions existing at the time the Emergency Law was implemented constituted the highest degree of public disorder and threatened Argentina's (D) security interests. Economic indicators were at catastrophic proportions, including GDP, unemployment, poverty, and indigence rates. The Government (D) was faced with a possible run on banks; there was looting and rioting and violent demonstrations; people were killed and conditions approached anarchy. All of these devastating economic, political, and social conditions together triggered the protections afforded under treaty to maintain order and control civil unrest. The treaty provisions in this regard are not triggered only by circumstances amounting to war or military action, since economic catastrophe can also wreak havoc on the lives of an entire population. Given these conditions, the Emergency Law was a reasonable response. Argentina's (D) conduct was also excused under customary international law, which excuses a state's international obligations during what is called a "state of necessity" or "state of emergency." Here, such a state of necessity existed in Argentina (D), as the country's very political and economic existence was seriously threatened. The Emergency Law, as part of an across-the-board response, was therefore necessary and reasonable, and Argentina (D) is exempted from liability.

▶ ANALYSIS

In rendering its opinion, the arbitral tribunal also found significant that the evidence did not show that Argentina's (D) actions contributed to the crisis that resulted in the state of necessity. Ostensibly, had Argentina (D) caused its own economic crisis through its deliberate actions, liability would not have been excused notwithstanding the state of emergency.

■■■

CMS v. Argentine Republic

U.S. company (P) v Foreign nation (D)

International Centre for the Settlement of Investment Disputes, ICSID Case No. ARB/01/8 (May 12, 2005).

NATURE OF CASE: Arbitral case brought under bilateral investment treaty (BIT).

FACT SUMMARY: [After Argentina (D) was found to have violated the U.S.-Argentina BIT based on its response to Argentina's (D) severe economic crisis, which response had the effect of drastically reducing the value of foreign investors' investments, Argentina (D) argued that its liability was excused by the BIT and by the customary international law doctrine of necessity.]

🏛 RULE OF LAW
A state's violation of a bilateral investment treaty is not excused under the doctrine of necessity where, although the state's response is to a severe crisis, the crisis does not result in total social and economic collapse, and government policies contributed significantly to the crisis.

FACTS: [In response to a severe economic crisis, Argentina (D) implemented various emergency measures in an attempt to stabilize its economy and prevent a state of anarchy and political and social upheaval and chaos. One of these measures was the so-called Emergency Law, which abolished peso-dollar convertibility, so that the one-to-one peg of the peso to the dollar no longer existed. In addition, the law terminated the right of privatized utilities, including gas companies, to payments calculated in dollars and the right to adjust those tariffs on the basis of the U.S. producer price index (PPI). The law forbade public utility companies from suspending or modifying compliance with their obligations under their concessions and licenses. The Emergency Law provided for a process of renegotiation of licenses to operate the gas transportation and distribution companies. Several attempts by the gas companies and the Government (D) to implement emergency increases in gas and electricity tariffs were blocked by the Argentine (D) courts. Some U.S. investors (P) brought arbitral cases, claiming that the Government's (D) measures produced devastating consequences for their investments and violated the U.S.-Argentina bilateral investment treaty (BIT). After Argentina (D) was found to have breached the BIT, Argentina (D) argued that its liability was excused by the customary international law doctrine of necessity as well as by the BIT itself, which provided that parties would not be precluded from applying measures necessary for the maintenance of public order and the protection of their security interests.]

ISSUE: Is a state's violation of a bilateral investment treaty excused under the doctrine of necessity where, although the state's response is to a severe crisis, the crisis does not

result in total social and economic collapse, and government policies contributed significantly to the crisis?

HOLDING AND DECISION: [Judge not stated in casebook excerpt.] No. A state's violation of a bilateral investment treaty is not excused under the doctrine of necessity where, although the state's response is to a severe crisis, the crisis does not result in total social and economic collapse, and government policies contributed significantly to the crisis. The excuse of necessity, while a part of customary international law, is exceptional and must be granted only rarely and upon strict review. Here, although the crisis was severe, Argentina's (D) wrongfulness may not be precluded as a matter of course. There was no grave and imminent peril that justified the wrongfulness, even though the Government (D) was justified in taking measures to prevent a worsening of the situation. There were alternatives to the measures taken, which clearly were not the "only way" for the Government (D) to protect its interests. Also, Argentina (D), through its government policies, contributed significantly to the crisis, which was exacerbated by exogenous factors. Finally, crises in other countries of similar magnitude have not led to the derogation of international contractual or treaty obligations. Accordingly, Argentina (D) may not be exempted from its responsibility under the BIT.

▶ ANALYSIS

The panel in this case, which awarded CMS millions of dollars in compensation, indicated that even if necessity had precluded the wrongfulness of Argentina's (D) acts, it would not have precluded Argentina's (D) responsibility to compensate CMS for its losses. Other tribunals have come out the other way on this issue, ruling that during a state of emergency the investor must bear its own damages.

■=■

CMS v. Argentine Republic

U.S. company (P) v Foreign nation (D)

International Centre for the Settlement of Investment Disputes,
ICSID Case No. ARB/01/8 (Sept. 25, 2007) (Annulment Proceeding).

NATURE OF CASE: Annulment proceeding in arbitral case brought under bilateral investment treaty (BIT).

FACT SUMMARY: [Argentina (D) sought the annulment of an award granted by an arbitral panel to CMS (P) for Argentina's (D) violations of a BIT.]

🏛 RULE OF LAW
Under the International Centre for the Settlement of Investment Disputes (ICSID) Convention, an arbitral award will not be annulled where the award has manifest errors of law but the arbitral panel has not exceeded its power.

FACTS: [Argentina (D) sought the annulment of an award granted by an arbitral panel to CMS (P) for Argentina's (D) violations of a BIT. As part of its decision, the arbitral panel ruled that Argentina's (D) violations during a severe economic crisis were not excused by the doctrine of necessity or by the BIT itself. The Committee reviewing the arbitral panel's award was bound by the ICSID Convention.]

ISSUE: Under the ICSID Convention, will an arbitral award be annulled where the award has manifest errors of law but the arbitral panel has not exceeded its power?

HOLDING AND DECISION: [Judge not stated in casebook excerpt.] No. Under the ICSID Convention, an arbitral award will not be annulled where the award has manifest errors of law but the arbitral panel has not exceeded its power. The jurisdiction of the Committee reviewing the award is limited by the provisions of the ICSID Convention, which clearly sets forth the criteria for annulment. The Committee is not an appeals court and does not have competence to overturn errors of law. Here, the panel (Tribunal) clearly erred by not analyzing whether a provision in the BIT relating to necessity was comparable to a similar provision in ILC's Articles on State Responsibility and whether both were applicable, since those provisions are substantively different in operation and content. Instead, the Tribunal merely assumed that the two provisions were on the same footing. Having failed to conduct such an analysis, the Tribunal made another error of law, namely that it failed to consider whether state of necessity in customary international law goes to the issue of wrongfulness or responsibility. In any event, the excuse based on customary law could only be subsidiary to the exclusion based on the BIT provision. If the Committee were acting as a court of appeal, it would have to reconsider the award on these grounds. But, since it is not a court of appeal, the Committee cannot substitute its own view of the law or the facts for those of the Tribunal, and, therefore, notwithstanding the Tribunal's errors or applying the BIT provision, it cannot be said that the Tribunal manifestly exceeded its powers. The award therefore will not be annulled.

▶ ANALYSIS

Annulment is concerned with the legitimacy of the decision-making process, not with the substantive correctness of the award. Article 52 of the ICSID Convention provides that annulment can occur on one or more of the following grounds:

(1) That the Tribunal was not properly constituted;

(2) That the Tribunal has manifestly exceeded its powers;

(3) That there was corruption on the part of a member of the Tribunal;

(4) That there has been a serious departure from a fundamental rule of procedure; or

(5) That the award has failed to state the reasons on which it is based.

Here, the Committee finds that none of these grounds was satisfied, and that even though there were errors of law, the arbitral panel did not violate subsection (b).

■—■

The Use of Force

Quick Reference Rules of Law

Case Concerning Military and Paramilitary Activities In and Against Nicaragua (Nicaragua v. United States)

Country aiding subversives (P) v. Military intervenor (D)

1986 I.C.J. 14 (June 27).

NATURE OF CASE: Action before the International Court of Justice.

FACT SUMMARY: [The United States (D) provided aid to the Contras, who were fighting the Marxist Sandinistas in Nicaragua. The United States (D) supplied financial, political, and military assistance to the Contras, who pursued their war against the Sandinistas from bases in neighboring Honduras and Costa Rica. In addition, U.S. military personnel or their agents covertly mined Nicaragua's harbors and carried out a number of attacks against Nicaraguan ports and military installations.] Nicaragua (P) sued the United States (D) for its actions against it. The United States (D) claimed its actions were justified based on the principle of collective self-defense insofar as it was aiding El Salvador stave off military aid from Nicaragua (P) to El Salvador opposition groups.

🏛 RULE OF LAW

(1) A state breaches the principle of nonintervention when, with a view to the coercion of another state, supports and assists armed bands in that other state whose purpose is to overthrow the government of that other state.

(2) It is a prima facie violation of the non-use of force principle for a state to participate in the acts of civil strife in another state by assisting an opposition group through encouraging the organization of irregular forces or armed bands.

(3) An assisting state's actions will not be considered justified collective self-defense against a purported armed attack where the "attack" consists merely of the provision of arms from the allegedly attacking state to the opposition in a third state and the third state has not officially declared itself the victim of an armed attack and has not asked for help from the assisting state.

(4) If one state acts towards another state in breach of the principle of nonintervention, but not through armed attack, a third state may not lawfully take such action by way of counter-measures against the first state as would otherwise constitute an intervention in its internal affairs.

(5) One state may not intervene against a second state on the ground that the latter has adopted a particular ideology or political system.

FACTS: [When the Sandinistas, a quasi-Marxist revolutionary front, took over the government of Nicaragua (P) the United States (D) began to support a group of Nicaraguan rebels, known as the Contras, in their efforts to overthrow the Sandinistas. The United States (D) supplied financial, political, and military assistance to the Contras, who pursued their war against the Sandinistas from bases in neighboring Honduras and Costa Rica. In addition, U.S. military personnel or their agents covertly mined Nicaragua's harbors and carried out a number of attacks against Nicaraguan ports and military installations. Nicaragua (P) filed suit against the United States (D) in the International Court of Justice (ICJ), asserting jurisdiction on the basis of each country's declaration under Article 36(2) of the Court's Statute, which permits the Court to hear any legal disputes between countries in accordance with the terms of their declarations, as well as on a provision in the 1956 Treaty of Friendship, Commerce, and Navigation between the two countries providing for ICJ resolution of disputes relating to the treaty. The United States (D), learning of Nicaragua's (P) intent to file the suit, attempted to modify its acceptance of the ICJ's Article 36(2) jurisdiction just a few days before the suit was filed. Relying on this attempted modification and a variety of other arguments, the United States (D) vigorously contested jurisdiction. When the Court ruled that it did have jurisdiction, the United States (D) refused to participate further in the case, and eventually terminated its acceptance of the Court's jurisdiction under Article 36(2). The court nevertheless proceeded to adjudge the merits of the case under customary international law as codified in the United Nations Charter.] Nicaragua (P) alleged that the actual use of force against it by the United States (D), including the laying of mines in Nicaraguan internal or territorial waters and attacks on Nicaraguan ports, oil installations and a naval base, as well as aiding military and paramilitary actions in and against Nicaragua (P) by the Contras was a violation of the non-use of force principle. The United States (D) claimed in public (but not before the Court) that its actions were justified as a collective self-defense against an armed attack by Nicaragua (P) against El Salvador. Nicaragua (P) was sending arms to opposition forces in El Salvador and the United States (D) claimed it was helping El Salvador in its self-defense.

ISSUE:

(1) Does a state breach the principle of non-intervention when, with a view to the coercion of another state, it supports and assists armed bands in that other state whose purpose is to overthrow the government of that other state?

(2) Is it a prima facie violation of the non-use of force principle for a state to participate in the acts of civil strife in

Continued on next page.

another state by assisting an opposition group through encouraging the organization of irregular forces or armed bands?

(3) Will an assisting state's actions be considered justified collective self-defense against a purported armed attack where the "attack" consists merely of the provision of arms from the allegedly attacking state to the opposition in a third state and the third state has not officially declared itself the victim of an armed attack and has not asked for help from the assisting state?

(4) If one state acts towards another state in breach of the principle of nonintervention, but not through armed attack, may a third state lawfully take such action by way of counter-measures against the first state as would otherwise constitute an intervention in its internal affairs?

(5) May, one state intervene against a second state on the ground that the latter has adopted a particular ideology or political system?

HOLDING AND DECISION: [Judge not stated in casebook excerpt.]

(1) Yes. A state breaches the principle of nonintervention when, with a view to the coercion of another state, it supports and assists armed bands in that other state whose purpose is to overthrow the government of that other state. Assistance to rebels in the form of provision of weapons or logistical support amounts to intervention in the internal affairs of another state. Nonintervention is a principle by which every sovereign state is entitled to conduct its affairs without outside interference. The principle of nonintervention forbids all states to intervene directly or indirectly in internal or external affairs of other states. A state is permitted to decide freely its political, economic, social, and cultural system and the formulation of foreign policy. Intervention is wrongful when it uses measures of coercion such as force either in the direct form of military action or in the indirect form of support for subversive or terrorist armed activities within another state. No right of intervention exists in support of opposition within another state and a breach will have occurred if a state supports directly, via military action, or indirectly, via support for subversive armed activities, within a state such intervention. On the other hand, merely imposing economic sanctions on another state does not constitute prohibited intervention. Finally, a request for intervention by a state's opposition does not justify such intervention, since if it did, this would permit any state to intervene at any moment in the internal affairs of another state, whether at the request of the government or at the request of its opposition.

(2) Yes. It is a prima facie violation of the non-use of force principle for a state to participate in the acts of civil strife in another state by assisting an opposition group through encouraging the organization of irregular forces or armed bands. The United States (D) committed a violation of the non-use of force principle by its assistance to the Contras

in Nicaragua by organizing or encouraging the organization of irregular forces or armed bands for incursion into the territory of Nicaragua and by participating in acts of civil strife in Nicaragua. Although the arming and training of the Contras involved the threat or use of force against Nicaragua (P), this was not necessarily so in respect of all the assistance given by the United States (D). For example, the mere supplying of funds to the Contras, while undoubtedly an act of intervention in the internal affairs of Nicaragua (P), did not in itself amount to a use of force.

(3) No. An assisting state's actions will not be considered justified collective self-defense against a purported armed attack where the "attack" consists merely of the provision of arms from the allegedly attacking state to the opposition in a third state and the third state has not officially declared itself the victim of an armed attack and has not asked for help from the assisting state. The United States' (D) actions were not justified in terms of self-defense because the provision of arms going to the opposition in El Salvador from Nicaragua (P) between 1979 and 1981 is not considered an armed attack, which necessarily must occur for the right of self defense to arise. While an armed attack may occur where armed bands or groups invade another state's territory to such an extent that the invasion is tantamount to an attack executed by armed forces, the mere provisions of weapons or logistical support to an opposition force does not qualify as an armed attack. Under customary international law, there is no rule permitting the exercise of collective self-defense in the absence of a request from the state that considers itself the victim of an armed attack, and there is also no rule that permits a non-victim state to exercise collective self-defense based solely on its own assessment of the situation. Further, it was not until 1984 that El Salvador officially declared itself the victim of an armed attack and asked the United States (D) to exercise the right of collective self-defense, which tends to prove that there was no armed attack in 1981 by Nicaragua (P). Moreover, the United States' (D) use of force—mining ports and attacking ports and oil installations—was disproportionate to whatever aid was being given to the opposition in El Salvador.

(4) No. If one state acts towards another state in breach of the principle of nonintervention, but not through armed attack, a third state may not lawfully take such action by way of counter-measures against the first state as would otherwise constitute an intervention in its internal affairs. Where an armed attack is involved, the third state might be justified in exercising collective self-defense, provided all the conditions justifying resort to such measures are present. However, where the intervention is less grave than an armed attack, only a proportionate response by the victim is justified, and counter-measures by a third state are not justified,

Continued on next page.

especially where those counter-measures involve the use of force.

(5) No. One state may not intervene against a second state on the ground that the latter has adopted a particular ideology or political system. The United States (D) was not justified in its actions based on its belief that Nicaragua (P) was a dictatorial communist regime or was violating human rights. Adherence by a state to any particular doctrine does not constitute a violation of customary international law; to hold otherwise would make nonsense of the fundamental principle of state sovereignty, on which the whole of international law rests, and the freedom of choice of the political, social, economic and cultural system of a state. Also, even if the United States (D) were attempting to ensure respect for human rights in Nicaragua (P), its response, involving the use of force, was not the appropriate method of ensuring such respect.

▶ ANALYSIS

Despite the Court's ruling for the United States (D) to desist immediately from further violations, the United States continued to support the Contras. Nicaragua (P) later agreed to hold internationally monitored elections in which a candidate who the United States (D) strongly supported was elected. Nicaragua (P) withdrew its suit prior to a decision on damages.

■■■■

Quicknotes

COERCION The overcoming of a person's free will as a result of threats, promises, or undue influence.

■■■■

Case Concerning Armed Activities on the Territory of the Congo (Democratic Republic of the Congo v. Uganda)

State (P) v. State (D)

2005 I.C.J. (Dec. 19).

NATURE OF CASE: Claim of armed aggression in violation of international law.

FACT SUMMARY: The Democratic Republic of the Congo (DRC) (P) charged that Uganda (D) violated international law and various agreements between the countries by engaging in military and paramilitary activity on DRC (P) territory.

🏛 RULE OF LAW

A state's aggression toward another state is not justified where the second state has not consented to the presence of the first state's troops on its territory and the first state is not acting in self-defense.

FACTS: [The Democratic Republic of the Congo (DRC) (P) accused Uganda (D) of "acts of armed aggression . . . in flagrant violation of the United Nations Charter and of the Charter of the Organization of African Unity," of providing "unlimited aid to rebels in the form of arms and armed troops, in return for the right to exploit the wealth of the Congo," and of gross violations of international humanitarian and human rights law. Uganda (D) counterclaimed, accusing the DRC (P) of acts of aggression and attacks on Ugandan (D) diplomatic premises and nationals in Kinshasa.] Uganda (D) argued that the DRC (P) consented to Uganda's (D) presence from May 1997 until September 11, 1998 (at which time Uganda stated that it decided to respond on the basis of self-defense), and that the DRC (P) renewed its consent on July 1999 through the Lusaka Agreement and subsequent amendments to the Lusaka Agreement. The Lusaka Agreement provided a calendar for withdrawal of Ugandan (D) troops from the DRC (P). Between September 11, 1998, and the July 1999 execution of the Lusaka Agreement, Uganda (D) argued, its military actions were self-defense. The DRC (P) claimed it did not attack Uganda (D).

ISSUE: Is a state's aggression toward another state justified where the second state has not consented to the presence of the first state's troops on its territory and the first state is not acting in self-defense?

HOLDING AND DECISION: [Judge not stated in casebook excerpt.] No. A state's aggression toward another state is not justified where the second state has not consented to the presence of the first state's troops on its territory and the first state is not acting in self-defense. The DRC (P) did not consent to the presence of Uganda's (D) troops on DRC (P) territory through international treaties, and Uganda's (D) aggression against the DRC (P) was not self-defense. First, the two parties agreed that their respective armies would cooperate in order to secure peace along the common border, but even though the language of the agreements evidenced consent by the DRC (P) to the presence of Ugandan (D) troops in the DRC (P), the consent was not open ended. Uganda's (D) military presence exceeded the timetable for agreed-upon withdrawal. In addition, the Lusaka Agreement—reached between the states in July 1999—does not refer to "consent," and does not constitute "an acceptance by all parties of Uganda's (D) justification for sending additional troops into the DRC (P) between mid-September 1998 and mid-July 1999," as Uganda (D) argued. The Lusaka arrangements were made to progress toward withdrawal of foreign forces and eventual peace. The DRC (P) did not consent to the presence of Ugandan (D) troops in the Lusaka Agreement, but simply concurred that there should be a process to end the turmoil in an orderly fashion. Nor did subsequent agreements modifying the Lusaka withdrawal timetable constitute consent to the presence of Ugandan (D) troops. Finally, while Uganda (D) claimed to have acted in self-defense, it did not ever claim that it had been subjected to an armed attack by the DRC (P), and there was no proof of DRC (P) involvement in any attacks against Uganda (D).

▶ ANALYSIS

The court interpreted the Lusaka Agreement—which referred to a calendar for withdrawal of "D-Day plus 180 days"—as not constituting consent by the DRC (P) to the presence of Ugandan (D) forces for at least 180 days from the date of execution, or "D-Day." If, as the court concluded, the DRC (P) did not consent to the presence of the troops for at least 180 days, then Uganda (D) had less than that amount of time to withdraw its troops, and the amount of time allowed for withdrawal could not be gleaned from the Lusaka Agreement calendar.

Legality of the Use of Force (Yugoslavia v. Belgium)

Sovereign state (P) v. Alleged aggressor state (D)

Oral Pleadings, CR/99/15 (1999).

NATURE OF CASE: Request before the International Court of Justice (ICJ) for provisional measures relating to armed aggression.

FACT SUMMARY: Member States of the North Atlantic Treaty Organization (NATO), including Belgium (D), engaged in a military campaign against the Federal Republic of Yugoslavia (FRY) (P) to force the FRY (P) and its Serb forces to negotiate a peace with Kosovar Albanians. The FRY (P) condemned NATO's actions as unlawful aggression and sought provisional measures.

🏛 **(PROPOSED) RULE OF LAW**
(1) Armed intervention by one state is justified to forestall an ongoing humanitarian catastrophe in another state.
(2) Armed intervention by one state is justified by a state of necessity in another state.

FACTS: Kosovo had been an autonomous province within the Republic of Serbia, itself a part of Yugoslavia (P). Kosovar Albanians constituted the majority in Kosovo and Serbs were its minority. When Slobodan Milosevic became the President of Serbia and the FRY (P), he revoked Kosovo's autonomy, and many Kosovars, including the Kosovo Liberation Army (KLA), employed insurrectionist tactics to regain independence. The FRY (P) response was further repression of the Kosovar Albanians. Outside parties (Western States) attempted to broker a peace that would involve interim autonomy for the Kosovars and full access by NATO troops to enforce the agreement. The Kosovars eventually accepted this agreement, but the FRY (P) did not. After negotiations broke down, the FRY (P) launched a spring offensive against the KLA and other Kosovars. A few days later, NATO began bombing selected targets in Kosovo and in Serbia. The FRY (P), instead of backing down, intensified its assault on the Kosovar Albanians. NATO's bombing campaign lasted several months. The UN's Security Council passed several resolutions demanding that the FRY (P) cease hostilities and withdraw its forces. Although it never expressly authorized the NATO campaign, the Council also did not condemn it. The FRY (P), on the other hand, did condemn the campaign as blatant aggression, and filed applications against all the NATO members: the United States, the United Kingdom, Spain, France, Germany, Italy, Netherlands, Canada, Portugal, and Belgium (D). The FRY (P) also sought provisional measures directing the NATO members to cease their use of force. To do so, the FRY (P) accepted the ICJ's jurisdiction retroactively and then brought its suits against the NATO member nations. The ICJ heard oral arguments.

ISSUE:
(1) Is armed intervention by one state justified to forestall an ongoing humanitarian catastrophe in another state?
(2) Is armed intervention by one state justified by a state of necessity in another state?

(PROPOSED) HOLDING AND DECISION:
(Oral arguments by Belgium.)

(1) Yes. Armed intervention by one state is justified to forestall an ongoing humanitarian catastrophe in another state. The Security Council's resolutions provide a basis for the armed intervention. Belgium (D) felt that it was obliged to intervene to forestall an ongoing humanitarian catastrophe acknowledged in those resolutions. The humanitarian values to be protected by such intervention are absolute rights and are, therefore, *jus cogens.* NATO did not intervene against FRY's (P) territorial independence or integrity; its purpose was to rescue a people in peril and deep distress. Such humanitarian intervention is compatible with Article 2, paragraph 4 of the UN Charter, and is also supported by precedent. Moreover, the NATO intervention was not condemned by the UN. Taken together, all these factors render the intervention legal. Still yet, there is a trend in international norms toward the protection of minorities from violent repression that takes precedence over concerns of state sovereignty. Finally, the action taken by NATO was also motivated by a desire to safeguard the stability of the entire region.

(2) Yes. Armed intervention by one state is justified by a state of necessity in another state. The notion of a state of necessity is a part of international law. This is a principle that says that there is a cause that justifies the violation of a binding rule in order to safeguard, in the face of grave and imminent peril, values that are higher than those protected by the rule that has been breached. The acts must also be proportionate. Applying this principle here, *arguendo,* there has been a breach of the rule against the use of force; the imminent peril is the humanitarian catastrophe recorded in the Security Council resolutions; the values are *jus cogens*—the collective security of an entire region; and, finally, the intervention is proportionate to the gravity of the peril—it was limited to aerial bombing directed solely at the aggressor's war machine and military-industrial complex.

▶ *ANALYSIS*

In response to Belgium's (D) state of necessity justification, arguments have been made that state of necessity may be

Continued on next page.

invoked only if the act at issue is the only means available and does not seriously impair an essential interest of the state owed the obligation. Here, the argument is that aerial bombing was not the only means available for the settlement of the dispute, but did impair an essential interest of the FRY (P). Additionally, the ICJ rejected jurisdiction on the grounds that the FRY's (P) consent to jurisdiction followed the timeframe of the dispute.

■═■

Quicknotes

ARGUENDO Hypothetical argument.

JUS COGENS NORM Universally understood principles of international law that cannot be set aside because they are based on fundamental human values.

SOVEREIGNTY The absolute power conferred to the State to govern and regulate all persons located and activities conducted therein.

■═■

CHAPTER 14

Challenges to International Law

Quick Reference Rules of Law

Kadi & Al Barakaat International v. Council of the European Union

Terrorists (D) v. European Union (P)

European Court of Justice, 3 CMLR 41 (2008).

NATURE OF CASE: Appeal of judgment by a European Community Court of First Instance.

FACT SUMMARY: [A regulation of the Council of the European Union (EU) (P) froze the funds of Yassin Abdullah Kadi (D) and Al Barakaat International Foundation (D), following a resolution by the U.N. Security Council. The EU Court of First Instance (CFI) ruled that it did not have jurisdiction to review measures adopted by the European Community (EC) giving effect to resolutions of the Security Council adopted against the Al Qaeda and Taliban terrorist networks.] Kadi (D) and Al Barakaat (D) appealed.

🏛 RULE OF LAW

The courts of the member states of the European Union (P) have jurisdiction to review measures adopted by the European Community that give effect to resolutions of the U.N. Security Council.

FACTS: [In its effort to fight terrorism, the U.N. Security Council imposed sanctions under Chapter VII of the U.N. Charter against individuals and entities allegedly associated with Osama bin Laden, the Al Qaeda network, and the Taliban. The U.N. Sanctions Committee made a list of alleged offenders, and sanctions included freezing such persons' and entities' assets. To give effect to the Security Council resolutions, the Council of the European Union (P) adopted a regulation ordering the freezing of the assets of those on the list, which included Yassin Abdullah Kadi (D), a resident of Saudi Arabia, and Al Barakaat International Foundation (D). Kadi (D) and Al Barakaat (D) began proceedings in the Court of First Instance (CFI) and requested annulment of the Council regulation, arguing that the Council lacked jurisdiction to adopt the regulation and that the regulation infringed several of their fundamental rights, including the right to respect for property, the right to be heard before a court of law, and the right to effective judicial review. The CFI rejected all claims and confirmed the validity of the regulation, ruling specifically that it had no jurisdiction to review the validity of the contested regulation and, indirectly, the validity of the relevant Security Council resolution, except in respect of jus cogens norms.] Kadi (D) and Al Barakaat (D) appealed.

ISSUE: Do the courts of the member states of the European Union (P) have jurisdiction to review measures adopted by the European Community that give effect to resolutions of the U.N. Security Council?

HOLDING AND DECISION: [Judge not stated in casebook excerpt.] Yes. The courts of the member states of the European Union (P) have jurisdiction to review measures adopted by the European Community that give effect to resolutions of the U.N. Security Council. EC courts have the power to review the legality of all Community acts, including the contested regulation, that aim to give effect to resolutions adopted by the Security Council under the U.N. Charter. The review of lawfulness applies only to the EC act purporting to give effect to the international agreement, not to the international agreement itself. Thus, EC courts do not have competence to review the legality of a resolution adopted by an international body, even if the courts limited their review to examination of the compatibility of that resolution with jus cogens norms. A judgment by an EU court that an EC measure is contrary to a higher rule of law in the EC legal order would not implicate a challenge to the legitimacy of that resolution in international law. Furthermore, the Sanctions Committee decisions are in essence diplomatic and intergovernmental, since only the government of an applicant's state of citizenship or residence may assert an applicant's rights and request removal from the list, and that Committee has no obligation to provide an individual with reasons as to why the individual appears on the list or for the Committee's rejection of an application for removal from the list. The Council regulation is annulled. Reversed.

▶ ANALYSIS

This case marks the first time that the ECJ confirmed its jurisdiction to review the lawfulness of a measure giving effect to Security Council resolutions. It also constitutes the first time the ECJ quashed an EC measure giving effect to a UNSC resolution for being unlawful.

Quicknotes

JUDICIAL REVIEW The authority of the courts to review decisions, actions, or omissions committed by another agency or branch of government.

JURISDICTION The authority of a court to hear and declare judgment in respect to a particular matter.

JUS COGENS NORM Universally understood principles of international law that cannot be set aside because they are based on fundamental human values.

Hamdi v. Rumsfeld

Suspected terrorist (P) v. Government official (D)

542 U.S. 507 (2004).

NATURE OF CASE: Appeal from dismissal of grant of habeas corpus petition.

FACT SUMMARY: Hamdi (P), a United States citizen who fought for the Taliban, claimed he was unlawfully detained by the U.S. government (D).

RULE OF LAW

The executive branch of the U.S. government is authorized to deter citizens who it suspects were part of or supporting forces hostile to the United States or coalition partners in Afghanistan and who engaged in armed conflict against the United States there.

FACTS: [Hamdi (P), a U.S. citizen, was captured in Afghanistan during the U.S. war against the Taliban. He was held without any charges at a naval prison in the United States. The Government (D) claimed that a declaration by a Department of Defense official explaining the Government's (D) views concerning the circumstances of Hamdi's (P) capture was a sufficient basis to hold a U.S. citizen caught in a zone of combat. More broadly, it asserted that the constitutional separation of powers required deference to the executive branch on military matters such as this determination. In the Government's (D) view, the Third Geneva Convention remained inapplicable pursuant to the President's determination, and, in any case, did not confer private rights of action on Hamdi (P). Hamdi (P) claimed he was unlawfully detained by the Government (D) and filed a habeas petition. The district court granted the petition, but the court of appeals reversed. The United States Supreme Court granted certiorari.]

ISSUE: Is the executive branch of the U.S. government authorized to deter citizens who it suspects were part of or supporting forces hostile to the United States or coalition partners in Afghanistan and who engaged in armed conflict against the United States there?

HOLDING AND DECISION: [O'Connor, J.] Yes. The executive branch of the U.S. government is authorized to deter citizens who it suspects were part of or supporting forces hostile to the United States or coalition partners in Afghanistan and who engaged in armed conflict against the United States there. Congress's Authorization for the Use of Military Force (AUMF) authorizes the President to use necessary force against nations associated with the terrorist attacks on September 11, 2001, and individuals who fought as part of the Taliban are individuals Congress sought to target in passing the AUMF. In addition, detention of lawful and unlawful combatants is an incident of war that is acceptable, though the law of war requires that detention may last no longer than active hostilities. [Vacated and remanded.]

▶ ANALYSIS

The U.S. government has claimed that no Taliban detainee is entitled to prisoner of war status. This would appear to be in violation of the Geneva Convention, which provides that where a prisoner's status is undetermined, the prisoner is entitled to "prisoner of war" status.

■■■

Quicknotes

GENEVA CONVENTION International agreement that governs the conduct of warring nations.

■■■

Hamdan v. Rumsfeld, Secretary of Defense

Detained terrorist (P) v. Government official (D)

548 U.S. 557 (2006).

NATURE OF CASE: Appeal from District Court holding that a military commission violated a detainee's rights under the Geneva Convention.

FACT SUMMARY: A U.S. military commission began proceedings against Hamdan (P), who was captured in Afghanistan. Hamdan (P) challenged the authority of the commission.

RULE OF LAW
The Geneva Convention does not create individual rights that are enforceable in U.S. federal courts.

FACTS: A U.S. military commission began proceedings against Hamdan (P), who was captured in Afghanistan. Hamdan (P) challenged the authority of the commission, arguing that the commission trial would violate his rights under Article 102 of the Geneva Convention, which provides that a "prisoner of war can be validly sentenced only if the sentence has been pronounced by the same courts according to the same procedure as in the case of members of the armed forces of the Detaining Power."

ISSUE: Does the Geneva Convention create individual rights that may are enforceable in U.S. federal courts?

HOLDING AND DECISION: [Judge not stated in casebook excerpt.] No. The Geneva Convention does not create individual rights that are enforceable in U.S. federal courts. First, Hamdan does not fit the Geneva Convention's definition of a prisoner of war, entitled to protection of the Convention, because he does not claim to be a member of a group who displayed insignia at a distance and who conducted operations in accordance with the laws of war. In addition, the 1949 Geneva Convention does not apply to al Qaeda and its members, because al Qaeda is not a state and was not a High Contracting party to the Convention, nor is the war against terrorism in general and the war against al Qaeda in particular a civil war. Even if Hamdan is protected by the Geneva Convention, the military commission procedures should not be tested against the Convention, because how the commission may try him is not a jurisdictional question; in that case, precedent requires deference to the ongoing military proceedings, and if Hamdan is convicted and if Common Article 3 covered him, he could contest his conviction in federal court after exhausting military remedies. In addition, the district court erred by holding that the military commissions created by the President must comply in all respects with the requirements of the Uniform Code of Military Justice (UCMJ). The UCMJ distinguishes between courts martial and military commissions, and most of the procedural rules in the UCMJ apply to courts martial, not

commissions. The more prudent limiting principle on the President's commissions is that he may not adopt procedures that are contrary to or inconsistent with the UCMJ's provisions governing military commissions.

CONCURRENCE: [Judge not stated in casebook excerpt.] Common Article 3 is properly read to apply to U.S. conduct. A conflict between a signatory and a non-state actor is a conflict not of international character, and the signatory is bound to Common Article 3's modest requirements of humane treatment and the judicial guarantees that are recognized as indispensable by civilized peoples.

▶ ANALYSIS

Many U.S. and international human rights organizations have determined that violations might occur through the non-application of the Geneva Convention to detainees in the U.S. war on terrorism.

■■■

Quicknotes

GENEVA CONVENTION International agreement that governs the conduct of warring nations.

■■■

Hamdan v. Rumsfeld, Secretary of State

Detained terrorist (P) v. Government official (D)

548 U.S. 557 (2006).

NATURE OF CASE: Appeal from reversal of grant of habeas petition in action challenging the authority of military tribunals to try alleged al Qaeda conspirators.

FACT SUMMARY: A U.S. military commission began proceedings against Hamdan (P), who was captured in Afghanistan and accused of conspiring with al Qaeda. Hamdan (P) challenged the authority of the commission.

🏛 RULE OF LAW

(1) The military commission established to try those deemed "enemy combatants" for alleged war crimes in the War on Terror was not authorized by the Congress or the inherent powers of the President.

(2) The rights protected by the Geneva Convention may be enforced in federal court through habeas corpus petitions.

FACTS: Hamdan (P) was captured in Afghanistan and imprisoned by the U.S. military at the Guantanamo detention center in Cuba. He was accused of conspiring with al Qaeda on the grounds that he was the driver and body guard of Osama bin Laden, and a U.S. military commission began proceedings against him, as he was designated an enemy combatant. Hamdan (P) brought a habeas petition, challenging the authority of the President to establish the military commission, and asserting that he was entitled to the Geneva Conventions' protections as a prisoner of war (POW). The district court granted Hamdan's (P) habeas petition, but the court of appeals reversed. The United States Supreme Court granted certiorari.

ISSUE:

(1) Was the military commission established to try those deemed "enemy combatants" for alleged war crimes in the War on Terror authorized by the Congress or the inherent powers of the President?

(2) May the rights protected by the Geneva Convention be enforced in federal court through habeas corpus petitions?

HOLDING AND DECISION: (Stevens, J.)

(1) No. The military commission established to try those deemed "enemy combatants" for alleged war crimes in the War on Terror was not authorized by the Congress or the inherent powers of the President. Neither an act of Congress nor the inherent powers of the executive branch laid out in the Constitution expressly authorized the sort of military commission at issue in this case. Absent that express authorization, the commission had to comply with the ordinary laws of the United States (D) and the laws of war.

(2) Yes. The rights protected by the Geneva Convention may be enforced in federal court through habeas corpus petitions. The Geneva Convention, as a part of the ordinary laws of war, could be enforced by the United States Supreme Court, along with the statutory Uniform Code of Military Justice (UCMJ), since the military commission was not authorized. Hamdan's (P) exclusion from certain parts of his trial deemed classified by the military commission violated both of these, and the trial was therefore illegal. Article 3 or "Common Article 3" as it is sometimes known, does apply to Hamdan (P), despite a holding to the contrary by the court of appeals, and arguments to the contrary by the Government (D). Common Article 3 provides minimal protection to individuals associated with neither a signatory nor a non-signatory "Power" who are involved in a conflict in the territory of a signatory. Common Article 3 is applicable here and requires that Hamdan (P) be tried by a "regularly constituted court affording all the judicial guarantees which are recognized as indispensable by civilized peoples." [Reversed and remanded.]

CONCURRENCE: (Kennedy, J.) Military Commission Order No. 1 represents a transgression by the Executive of Congress's express limits. Because Congress has spoken on this matter, the Executive's powers are at their lowest, so that the President may not establish military commissions in contravention of Congress's will on the basis of Executive power.

DISSENT: (Thomas, J.) The President should be accorded great deference in matters of national defense. Based on al Qaeda's actions before and after 9/11, the conspiracy charge was justified, and conspiracy with, or membership in, an organization such as al Qaeda that engages in violations of the laws of war are crimes that may be tried by military commissions. This occurred in Nuremberg after World War II. Moreover, the President's determinations under Article 36 of the UCMJ must be deferred to, and the Geneva Conventions may not be relied on in U.S. law. Even if the Conventions could be looked to, in any event Common Article 3 is inapplicable to al Qaeda.

DISSENT: (Alito, J.) Military commissions come within Common Article 3's scope. First, that article requires a court. Here, the military commissions qualify as courts. The second requirement, that the court be "regularly constituted" is also met. This requires that the court be appointed or established in accordance with the appointing country's

Continued on next page.

domestic law. Here, the commissions were established in accordance with such domestic law since they were established by the President in the lawful exercise of his executive powers. The majority errs in holding that a military commission cannot be regarded as "a regularly constituted court" unless it is similar in structure and composition to a regular military court or unless there is an "evident practical need" for the divergence therefrom. These requirements do not negate the fact that the commissions are still "regularly constituted." Even if Common Article 3 recognizes a prohibition on "special tribunals," that prohibition does not cover the military commissions here because "special" would mean "relating to a single thing," and "regular" would mean "uniform in course, practice, or occurrence." Insofar as the Government (D) proposes to conduct the tribunals according to the procedures of Military Commission Order No. 1, then it seems that Hamdan's (P) tribunal, like the hundreds of others the Government (D) propose to conduct, is very much regular and not at all special. Finally, the article requires that the court proceeding afford "all the judicial guarantees which are recognized as indispensable by civilized peoples." This requirement is also met because the availability of review by a United States Court of Appeals and by the Supreme Court does not provide a basis for deeming the commissions to be illegitimate. This view is supported by the commentary to the article, which indicated that the article was intended to prohibit "summary justice." The military commissions, with their formal trial procedures and the availability of multiple levels of review, do not dispense summary justice.

▶ *ANALYSIS*

Many U.S. and international human rights organizations have determined that violations might occur through the non-application of the Geneva Convention to detainees in the U.S. war on terrorism.

■═■

Quicknotes

GENEVA CONVENTION International agreement that governs the conduct of warring nations.

HABEAS CORPUS A proceeding in which a defendant brings a writ to compel a judicial determination of whether he is lawfully being held in custody.

■═■

Public Committee Against Torture in Israel v. Government of Israel

Non-governmental organization (P) v. State (D)

Israel Sup. Ct., http://elyon1.court.gov.il/files_eng/02/690/007/A34/02007690.a34.pdf (2005).

NATURE OF CASE: Action claiming violations of international humanitarian and human rights laws.

FACT SUMMARY: [Non-governmental organizations (NGOs) (P) brought suit against Israel (D), claiming that its practice of preemptive targeted killings of suspected terrorists violated international humanitarian and human rights laws.]

RULE OF LAW

Not all preemptive targeted killings of suspected terrorists violate customary international humanitarian and human rights laws where the laws of armed conflict apply.

FACTS: [Since 2000, the Israeli military killed around 210 people in the West Bank and Gaza Strip. Israel (D) asserted that these individuals were leading terrorists representing an immediate threat to Israeli civilians and that they could not be arrested. At least 125 innocent civilians were killed in these operations. NGOs (P) brought suit against Israel (D), claiming that this practice of preemptive targeted killings of suspected terrorists constituted illegal extrajudicial killing under international human rights law and, in the alternative, impermissible killing of civilians under international humanitarian law. The Israeli Supreme Court rendered its opinion in the case, affirming its earlier opinions that an international armed conflict existed between Israeli and terrorist organizations in the West Bank and Gaza and thus that only the law of armed conflict applied.]

ISSUE: Do all preemptive targeted killings of suspected terrorists violate customary international humanitarian and human rights laws where the laws of armed conflict apply?

HOLDING AND DECISION: [Judge not stated in casebook excerpt.] No. Not all preemptive targeted killings of suspected terrorists violate customary international humanitarian and human rights laws where the laws of armed conflict apply. The terrorists at issue do not fall within the criteria for combatants under the Hague Regulations, §1, as they do not belong to the armed forces and do not belong to units to which international law grants status similar to that of combatants. They are unlawful combatants and are entitled to minimum protections offered by customary international law. Under international law, if one is not a combatant, one is a civilian, so that even unlawful combatants are civilians. The question then becomes whether such unlawful combatant-civilians are entitled to the same protections as civilians who are not unlawful combatants. The answer is "no," since customary international law deems a civilian taking a direct part in hostilities as not entitled to protections from attack granted civilians who are not engaged directly in hostilities. Thus, these unlawful combatant terrorists are civilians who are not protected from attack as long as they take a direct part in the hostilities. They are not, under Hague and Geneva Conventions, in a separate third category of "unlawful combatant." Currently under international law there is no room in the existing framework for such a category. Thus, while the unlawful combatant-civilian is not protected from attack while directly participating in hostilities, he or she also does not enjoy the rights of a combatant, such as those granted to a prisoner of war. Currently, in this context, "hostilities" are viewed as acts intended to cause damage to armed forces, but this definition should be broadened to include acts intended to harm civilians. Under the accepted definition, a civilian takes part in hostilities when using weapons in an armed conflict, while gathering intelligence, or while preparing for the hostilities. However, there is no accepted definition of "direct" in this context, so that the term must be determined on a case-by-case basis. It is clear that one who is armed and going to a place to use weapons against an army is directly participating in hostilities. It is also clear that one who generally supports the hostilities, or who sells food or medicine to unlawful combatants, is taking an only indirect part in the hostilities. Other instances of direct participation include: collecting intelligence on the army; transporting unlawful combatants to or from the locus of hostilities; operating weapons used by the unlawful combatants or supervising their operation, or providing services to them, regardless of how far away from the battlefield these providers of ancillary support may be. Those who send the unlawful combatants, who have decided on the attack, or who planned it are also direct participants. On the other hand, it is not direct participation to aid unlawful combatants with general strategic analysis, or logistical support and money. Another factor that needs determination is the period during which an unlawful combatant-civilian is not entitled to protection from attack. There is no consensus on this issue. A civilian who engages in a single act of hostilities is entitled to protection from attack after his act of hostility is over, and is not to be attacked for hostilities he committed in the past. On the other hand, a civilian who has joined a terrorist group and regularly engages in hostile acts loses immunity from attack for as long as he is engaging in the hostile acts, even if there are periods of rest between such acts. In this regard, each case must be determined on its own merits. This requires sound information, and the burden on the attacking army is heavy. If there is any doubt that a civilian is a terrorist, careful verification is needed before an attack on that individual may be made. Also, an unlawful combatant may not be attacked if a less harmful means can be employed—such as

Continued on next page.

arrest, interrogation, and trial. Additionally, where harm to nearby innocent civilians from the use of force would be greater than that caused by refraining from it, it should not be used. Moreover, after an attack, a thorough, independent and retroactive investigation must be made regarding the precision of the identification of the target and the circumstances of the attack. Compensation should be paid, where appropriate, as a result of the harm caused to innocent civilians. Such collateral damage must withstand a test of proportionality, determined according to a values-based test, intended to balance between the military advantage and the civilian damage. Accordingly, it cannot be said that every preventative strike is permitted or forbidden; it depends on the circumstances of each particular strike. Killing suspected terrorists is permitted on condition that there is no other means which harms them less, and on condition that innocent civilians are not harmed, or, where there is harm, that the damage is proportional.

▶ *ANALYSIS*

The principle of proportionality is difficult to implement. When dealing with it in advance, under time constraints, and in light of a limited amount of information, the decision to make a preemptive strike is likely to be difficult and complex. It is often necessary to consider values and attributes that are not easily compared. Moreover, each of the competing considerations is itself subject to relative variables, and none of them can be considered standing alone. The proportionate military need includes humanitarian elements, while the scope of the humanitarian consideration often includes existential military need. Courts will determine the law applying to the decision of the military commander, and will ask whether a reasonable military commander would have made the decision which was actually made, in light of the normative systems that apply to the case.

■■■

Glossary

Common Latin Words and Phrases Encountered in the Law

A FORTIORI: Because one fact exists or has been proven, therefore a second fact that is related to the first fact must also exist.

A PRIORI: From the cause to the effect. A term of logic used to denote that when one generally accepted truth is shown to be a cause, another particular effect must necessarily follow.

AB INITIO: From the beginning; a condition which has existed throughout, as in a marriage which was void ab initio.

ACTUS REUS: The wrongful act; in criminal law, such action sufficient to trigger criminal liability.

AD VALOREM: According to value; an ad valorem tax is imposed upon an item located within the taxing jurisdiction calculated by the value of such item.

AMICUS CURIAE: Friend of the court. Its most common usage takes the form of an amicus curiae brief, filed by a person who is not a party to an action but is nonetheless allowed to offer an argument supporting his legal interests.

ARGUENDO: In arguing. A statement, possibly hypothetical, made for the purpose of argument, is one made arguendo.

BILL QUIA TIMET: A bill to quiet title (establish ownership) to real property.

BONA FIDE: True, honest, or genuine. May refer to a person's legal position based on good faith or lacking notice of fraud (such as a bona fide purchaser for value) or to the authenticity of a particular document (such as a bona fide last will and testament).

CAUSA MORTIS: With approaching death in mind. A gift causa mortis is a gift given by a party who feels certain that death is imminent.

CAVEAT EMPTOR: Let the buyer beware. This maxim is reflected in the rule of law that a buyer purchases at his own risk because it is his responsibility to examine, judge, test, and otherwise inspect what he is buying.

CERTIORARI: A writ of review. Petitions for review of a case by the United States Supreme Court are most often done by means of a writ of certiorari.

CONTRA: On the other hand. Opposite. Contrary to.

CORAM NOBIS: Before us; writs of error directed to the court that originally rendered the judgment.

CORAM VOBIS: Before you; writs of error directed by an appellate court to a lower court to correct a factual error.

CORPUS DELICTI: The body of the crime; the requisite elements of a crime amounting to objective proof that a crime has been committed.

CUM TESTAMENTO ANNEXO, ADMINISTRATOR (ADMINISTRATOR C.T.A.): With will annexed; an administrator c.t.a. settles an estate pursuant to a will in which he is not appointed.

DE BONIS NON, ADMINISTRATOR (ADMINISTRATOR D.B.N.): Of goods not administered; an administrator d.b.n. settles a partially settled estate.

DE FACTO: In fact; in reality; actually. Existing in fact but not officially approved or engendered.

DE JURE: By right; lawful. Describes a condition that is legitimate "as a matter of law," in contrast to the term "de facto," which connotes something existing in fact but not legally sanctioned or authorized. For example, de facto segregation refers to segregation brought about by housing patterns, etc., whereas de jure segregation refers to segregation created by law.

DE MINIMIS: Of minimal importance; insignificant; a trifle; not worth bothering about.

DE NOVO: Anew; a second time; afresh. A trial de novo is a new trial held at the appellate level as if the case originated there and the trial at a lower level had not taken place.

DICTA: Generally used as an abbreviated form of obiter dicta, a term describing those portions of a judicial opinion incidental or not necessary to resolution of the specific question before the court. Such nonessential statements and remarks are not considered to be binding precedent.

DUCES TECUM: Refers to a particular type of writ or subpoena requesting a party or organization to produce certain documents in their possession.

EN BANC: Full bench. Where a court sits with all justices present rather than the usual quorum.

EX PARTE: For one side or one party only. An ex parte proceeding is one undertaken for the benefit of only one party, without notice to, or an appearance by, an adverse party.

EX POST FACTO: After the fact. An ex post facto law is a law that retroactively changes the consequences of a prior act.

EX REL.: Abbreviated form of the term "ex relatione," meaning upon relation or information. When the state brings an action in which it has no interest against an individual at the instigation of one who has a private interest in the matter.

FORUM NON CONVENIENS: Inconvenient forum. Although a court may have jurisdiction over the case, the action should be tried in a more conveniently located court, one to which parties and witnesses may more easily travel, for example.

GUARDIAN AD LITEM: A guardian of an infant as to litigation, appointed to represent the infant and pursue his/her rights.

HABEAS CORPUS: You have the body. The modern writ of habeas corpus is a writ directing that a person (body) being detained (such as a prisoner) be brought before the court so that the legality of his detention can be judicially ascertained.

IN CAMERA: In private, in chambers. When a hearing is held before a judge in his chambers or when all spectators are excluded from the courtroom.

IN FORMA PAUPERIS: In the manner of a pauper. A party who proceeds in forma pauperis because of his poverty is one who is allowed to bring suit without liability for costs.

INFRA: Below, under. A word referring the reader to a later part of a book. (The opposite of supra.)

IN LOCO PARENTIS: In the place of a parent.

IN PARI DELICTO: Equally wrong; a court of equity will not grant requested relief to an applicant who is in pari delicto, or as much at fault in the transactions giving rise to the controversy as is the opponent of the applicant.

IN PARI MATERIA: On like subject matter or upon the same matter. Statutes relating to the same person or things are said to be in pari materia. It is a general rule of statutory construction that such statutes should be construed together, i.e., looked at as if they together constituted one law.

IN PERSONAM: Against the person. Jurisdiction over the person of an individual.

IN RE: In the matter of. Used to designate a proceeding involving an estate or other property.

IN REM: A term that signifies an action against the res, or thing. An action in rem is basically one that is taken directly against property, as distinguished from an action in personam, i.e., against the person.

INTER ALIA: Among other things. Used to show that the whole of a statement, pleading, list, statute, etc., has not been set forth in its entirety.

INTER PARTES: Between the parties. May refer to contracts, conveyances or other transactions having legal significance.

INTER VIVOS: Between the living. An inter vivos gift is a gift made by a living grantor, as distinguished from bequests contained in a will, which pass upon the death of the testator.

IPSO FACTO: By the mere fact itself.

JUS: Law or the entire body of law.

LEX LOCI: The law of the place; the notion that the rights of parties to a legal proceeding are governed by the law of the place where those rights arose.

MALUM IN SE: Evil or wrong in and of itself; inherently wrong. This term describes an act that is wrong by its very nature, as opposed to one which would not be wrong but for the fact that there is a specific legal prohibition against it (malum prohibitum).

MALUM PROHIBITUM: Wrong because prohibited, but not inherently evil. Used to describe something that is wrong because it is expressly forbidden by law but that is not in and of itself evil, e.g., speeding.

MANDAMUS: We command. A writ directing an official to take a certain action.

MENS REA: A guilty mind; a criminal intent. A term used to signify the mental state that accompanies a crime or other prohibited act. Some crimes require only a general mens rea (general intent to do the prohibited act), but others, like assault with intent to murder, require the existence of a specific mens rea.

MODUS OPERANDI: Method of operating; generally refers to the manner or style of a criminal in committing crimes, admissible in appropriate cases as evidence of the identity of a defendant.

NEXUS: A connection to.

NISI PRIUS: A court of first impression. A nisi prius court is one where issues of fact are tried before a judge or jury.

N.O.V. (NON OBSTANTE VEREDICTO): Notwithstanding the verdict. A judgment n.o.v. is a judgment given in favor of one party despite the fact that a verdict was returned in favor of the other party, the justification being that the verdict either had no reasonable support in fact or was contrary to law.

NUNC PRO TUNC: Now for then. This phrase refers to actions that may be taken and will then have full retroactive effect.

PENDENTE LITE: Pending the suit; pending litigation under way.

PER CAPITA: By head; beneficiaries of an estate, if they take in equal shares, take per capita.

PER CURIAM: By the court; signifies an opinion ostensibly written "by the whole court" and with no identified author.

PER SE: By itself, in itself; inherently.

PER STIRPES: By representation. Used primarily in the law of wills to describe the method of distribution where a person, generally because of death, is unable to take that which is left to him by the will of another, and therefore his heirs divide such property between them rather than take under the will individually.

PRIMA FACIE: On its face, at first sight. A prima facie case is one that is sufficient on its face, meaning that the evidence supporting it is adequate to establish the case until contradicted or overcome by other evidence.

PRO TANTO: For so much; as far as it goes. Often used in eminent domain cases when a property owner receives partial payment for his land without prejudice to his right to bring suit for the full amount he claims his land to be worth.

QUANTUM MERUIT: As much as he deserves. Refers to recovery based on the doctrine of unjust enrichment in those cases in which a party has rendered valuable services or furnished materials that were accepted and enjoyed by another under circumstances that would reasonably notify the recipient that the rendering party expected to be paid. In essence, the law implies a contract to pay the reasonable value of the services or materials furnished.

QUASI: Almost like; as if; nearly. This term is essentially used to signify that one subject or thing is almost analogous to another but that material differences between them do exist. For example, a quasi-criminal proceeding is one that is not strictly criminal but shares enough of the same characteristics to require some of the same safeguards (e.g., procedural due process must be followed in a parole hearing).

QUID PRO QUO: Something for something. In contract law, the consideration, something of value, passed between the parties to render the contract binding.

RES GESTAE: Things done; in evidence law, this principle justifies the admission of a statement that would otherwise be hearsay when it is made so closely to the event in question as to be said to be a part of it, or with such spontaneity as not to have the possibility of falsehood.

RES IPSA LOQUITUR: The thing speaks for itself. This doctrine gives rise to a rebuttable presumption of negligence when the instrumentality causing the injury was within the exclusive control of the defendant, and the injury was one that does not normally occur unless a person has been negligent.

RES JUDICATA: A matter adjudged. Doctrine which provides that once a court of competent jurisdiction has rendered a final judgment or decree on the merits, that judgment or decree is conclusive upon the parties to the case and prevents them from engaging in any other litigation on the points and issues determined therein.

RESPONDEAT SUPERIOR: Let the master reply. This doctrine holds the master liable for the wrongful acts of his servant (or the principal for his agent) in those cases in which the servant (or agent) was acting within the scope of his authority at the time of the injury.

STARE DECISIS: To stand by or adhere to that which has been decided. The common law doctrine of stare decisis attempts to give security and certainty to the law by following the policy that once a principle of law as applicable to a certain set of facts has been set forth in a decision, it forms a precedent which will subsequently be followed, even though a different decision might be made were it the first time the question had arisen. Of course, stare decisis is not an inviolable principle and is departed from in instances where there is good cause (e.g., considerations of public policy led the Supreme Court to disregard prior decisions sanctioning segregation).

SUPRA: Above. A word referring a reader to an earlier part of a book.

ULTRA VIRES: Beyond the power. This phrase is most commonly used to refer to actions taken by a corporation that are beyond the power or legal authority of the corporation.

Addendum of French Derivatives

IN PAIS: Not pursuant to legal proceedings.

CHATTEL: Tangible personal property.

CY PRES: Doctrine permitting courts to apply trust funds to purposes not expressed in the trust but necessary to carry out the settlor's intent.

PER AUTRE VIE: For another's life; during another's life. In property law, an estate may be granted that will terminate upon the death of someone other than the grantee.

PROFIT A PRENDRE: A license to remove minerals or other produce from land.

VOIR DIRE: Process of questioning jurors as to their predispositions about the case or parties to a proceeding in order to identify those jurors displaying bias or prejudice.

Casenote Legal Briefs